The Silver Lining: Moral Deliberations in Modern Films

6th EDITION

Sam Vaknin, Ph.D.

Editing and Design:
Lidija Rangelovska

*Lidija Rangelovska
A Narcissus Publications Imprint, Skopje 2018*

© 2002-18 Copyright Lidija Rangelovska.

All rights reserved. This book, or any part thereof, may not be used or reproduced in any manner without written permission from:

Lidija Rangelovska – write to:

palma@unet.com.mk

Philosophical Musings and Essays

http://samvak.tripod.com/culture.html

Malignant Self-love: Narcissism Revisited

http://www.narcissistic-abuse.com

Created by: LIDIJA RANGELOVSKA
REPUBLIC OF MACEDONIA

CONTENTS

I.	The Talented Mr. Ripley
II.	The Truman Show
III.	The Matrix
IV.	Shattered
V.	Titanic
VI.	Being John Malkovich
VII.	Dreamcatcher: The Myth of Destructibility
VIII.	I, Robot: The Fourth Law of Robotics
IX.	Surrogates: The Interrupted Self
X.	Avatar: The Ecology of Environmentalism
XI.	The Invention of Lying: Fact and Truth
XII.	Hostel: The American Hostel
XIII.	Inceptions and Its Errors
XIV.	Aliens 'R Us: The Ten Errors of Science Fiction
XV.	Loving Gaze, Adulating Gaze ("The Beaver")
XVI.	The Malignant Optimism of the Abused ("We Need to Talk about Kevin")
XVII.	The Disruptive Engine: Innovation ("The Artist")
XVIII.	What to Expect When You Are Expecting
XIX.	Her and Interspecies Romance
XX.	The Last Tango in Paris
XXI.	The Best Offer
XXII.	The Place
XXIII.	The Author
XXIV.	About "After the Rain"

The Talented Mr. Ripley

"The Talented Mr. Ripley" is an Hitchcockian and blood-curdling study of the psychopath and his victims. At the centre of this masterpiece, set in the exquisitely decadent scapes of Italy, is a titanic encounter between Ripley, the aforementioned psychopath protagonist and young Greenleaf, a consummate narcissist.

Ripley is a cartoonishly poor young adult whose overriding desire is to belong to a higher - or at least, richer - social class. While he waits upon the subjects of his not so hidden desires, he receives an offer he cannot refuse: to travel to Italy to retrieve the spoiled and hedonistic son of a shipbuilding magnate, Greenleaf Senior. He embarks upon a study of Junior's biography, personality, likes and hobbies. In a chillingly detailed process, he actually assumes Greenleaf's identity. Disembarking from a luxurious Cunard liner in his destination, Italy, he "confesses" to a gullible textile-heiress that he is the young Greenleaf, travelling incognito.

Thus, we are subtly introduced to the two over-riding themes of the antisocial personality disorder (still labelled by many professional authorities "psychopathy" and "sociopathy"): an overwhelming dysphoria and an even more overweening drive to assuage this angst by belonging. The psychopath is an unhappy person. He is besieged by recurrent depression bouts, hypochondria and an overpowering sense of alienation and drift. He is bored with his own life and is permeated by a seething and explosive envy of the lucky, the mighty, the clever, the have it alls, the know it alls, the handsome, the happy - in short: his opposites. He feels discriminated against and dealt a poor hand in the great poker game called life. He is driven obsessively to right these perceived wrongs and feels entirely justified in adopting whatever means he deems necessary in pursuing this goal.

Ripley's reality test is maintained throughout the film. In other words - while he gradually merges with the object of his admiring emulation, the young Greenleaf - Ripley can always tell the difference. After he kills Greenleaf in self-defense, he assumes his name, wears his clothes, cashes his checks and makes phone calls from his rooms. But he also murders - or tries to murder - those who suspect the truth. These acts of lethal self-preservation prove conclusively that he knows who he is and that he fully realizes that his acts are parlously illegal.

Young Greenleaf is young, captivatingly energetic, infinitely charming, breathtakingly handsome and deceivingly emotional. He lacks real talents - he know how to play only six jazz tunes, can't make up his musical mind between his faithful sax and a newly alluring drum kit and, an aspiring writer, can't even spell. These shortcomings and discrepancies are tucked under a glittering facade of nonchalance, refreshing spontaneity, an experimental spirit, unrepressed sexuality and unrestrained adventurism. But Greenleaf Jr. is a garden variety narcissist. He cheats on his lovely and loving girlfriend, Marge. He refuses to lend money - of which he seems to have an unlimited supply, courtesy his ever more disenchanted father - to a girl he impregnated. She commits suicide and he blames the primitiveness of the emergency services, sulks and kicks his precious record player. In the midst of this infantile temper tantrum the rudiments of a conscience are visible. He evidently feels guilty. At least for a while.

Greenleaf Jr. falls in and out of love and friendship in a predictable pendulous rhythm. He idealizes his beaus and then devalues them. He finds them to be the quiddity of fascination one moment - and the distilled essence of boredom the next. And he is not shy about expressing his distaste and disenchantment. He is savagely cruel as he calls Ripley a leach who has taken over his life and his possessions (having previously invited him to do so in no uncertain terms). He says that he is relieved to see him go and he cancels off-handedly elaborate plans they made together. Greenleaf Jr. maintains a poor record of keeping promises and a rich record of violence, as we discover towards the end of this suspenseful, taut yarn.

Ripley himself lacks an identity. He is a binary automaton driven by a set of two instructions - become someone and overcome resistance. He feels like a nobody and his overriding ambition is to be somebody, even if he has to fake it, or steal it. His only talents, he openly admits, are to fake both personalities and papers. He is a predator and he hunts for congruence, cohesion and meaning. He is in constant search of a family. Greenleaf Jr., he declares festively, is the older brother he never had. Together with the long suffering fiancee in waiting, Marge, they are a family. Hasn't Greenleaf Sr. actually adopted him?

This identity disturbance, which is at the psychodynamic root of both pathological narcissism and rapacious psychopathy, is all-pervasive. Both Ripley and Greenleaf Jr. are not sure who they are. Ripley wants to be Greenleaf Jr. - not because of the latter's admirable personality, but because of his money. Greenleaf Jr. cultivates a False Self of a jazz giant in the making and the author of the Great American Novel but he is neither and he bitterly knows it. Even their sexual identity is not fully formed. Ripley is at once homoerotic, autoerotic and heteroerotic. He has a succession of homosexual lovers (though apparently only platonic ones). Yet, he is attracted to women. He falls desperately in love with Greenleaf's False Self and it is the revelation of the latter's dilapidated True Self that leads to the atavistically bloody scene in the boat.

But Ripley is a different -and more ominous - beast altogether. He rambles on about the metaphorical dark chamber of his secrets, the key to which he wishes to share with a "loved" one. But this act of sharing (which never materializes) is intended merely to alleviate the constant pressure of the hot pursuit he is subjected to by the police and others. He disposes with equal equanimity of both loved ones and the occasional prying acquaintance. At least twice he utters words of love as he actually strangles his newfound inamorato and tries to slash an old and rekindled flame. He hesitates not a split second when confronted with an offer to betray Greenleaf Sr., his nominal employer and benefactor, and abscond with his money. He falsifies signatures with ease, makes eye contact convincingly, flashes the most heart rending smile when embarrassed or endangered. He is a caricature of the American dream: ambitious, driven, winsome, well versed in the mantras of the bourgeoisie. But beneath this thin veneer of hard learned, self-conscious and uneasy civility - lurks a beast of prey best characterized by the DSM IV (Diagnostic and Statistics Manual):

"Failure to conform to social norms with respect to lawful behaviour, deceitfulness as indicated by repeated lying, use of aliases, or conning others to personal profit or pleasure, impulsivity or failure to plan ahead... reckless disregard for safety of self or others ...(and above all) lack of remorse." (From the criteria of the Antisocial Personality Disorder).

But perhaps the most intriguing portraits are those of the victims. Marge insists, in the face of the most callous and abusive behaviour, that there is something "tender" in Greenleaf Jr. When she confronts the beguiling monster, Ripley, she encounters the fate of all victims of psychopaths: disbelief, pity and ridicule. The truth is too horrible to contemplate, let alone comprehend. Psychopaths are inhuman in the most profound sense of this compounded word. Their emotions and conscience have been amputated and replaced by phantom imitations. But it is rare to pierce their meticulously crafted facade. They more often than not go on to great success and social acceptance while their detractors are relegated to the fringes of society. Both Meredith and Peter, who had the misfortune of falling in deep, unrequited love with Ripley, are punished. One by losing his life, the other by losing Ripley time and again, mysteriously, capriciously, cruelly.

Thus, ultimately, the film is an intricate study of the pernicious ways of psychopathology. Mental disorder is a venom not confined to its source. It spreads and affects its environment in a myriad surreptitiously subtle forms. It is a hydra, growing one hundred heads where one was severed. Its victims writhe and as abuse is piled upon trauma - they turn to stone, the mute witnesses of horror, the stalactites and stalagmites of pain untold and unrecountable. For their tormentors are often as talented as Mr. Ripley is and they are as helpless and as clueless as his victims are.

Return

The Truman Show

"The Truman Show" is a profoundly disturbing movie. On the surface, it deals with the worn out issue of the intermingling of life and the media.

Examples for such incestuous relationships abound:

Ronald Reagan, the cinematic president was also a presidential movie star. In another movie ("The Philadelphia Experiment") a defrosted Rip Van Winkle exclaims upon seeing Reagan on television (40 years after his forced hibernation started): "I know this guy, he used to play Cowboys in the movies".

Candid cameras monitor the lives of webmasters (website owners) almost 24 hours a day. The resulting images are continuously posted on the Web and are available to anyone with a computer.

The last decade witnessed a spate of films, all concerned with the confusion between life and the imitations of life, the media. The ingenious "Capitan Fracasse", "Capricorn One", "Sliver", "Wag the Dog" and many lesser films have all tried to tackle this (un)fortunate state of things and its moral and practical implications.

The blurring line between life and its representation in the arts is arguably the main theme of "The Truman Show". The hero, Truman, lives in an artificial world, constructed especially for him. He was born and raised there. He knows no other place. The people around him – unbeknownst to him – are all actors. His life is monitored by 5000 cameras and broadcast live to the world, 24 hours a day, every day. He is spontaneous and funny because he is unaware of the monstrosity of which he is the main cogwheel.

But Peter Weir, the movie's director, takes this issue one step further by perpetrating a massive act of immorality on screen. Truman is lied to, cheated, deprived of his ability to make choices, controlled and manipulated by sinister, half-mad Shylocks. As I said, he is unwittingly the only spontaneous, non-scripted, "actor" in the on-going soaper of his own life. All the other figures in his life, including his parents, are actors. Hundreds of millions of viewers and voyeurs plug in to take a peep, to intrude upon what Truman innocently and honestly believes to be his privacy. They are shown responding to various dramatic or anti-climactic events in Truman's life. That we are the moral equivalent of these viewers-voyeurs, accomplices to the same crimes, comes as a shocking realization to us. We are (live) viewers and they are (celluloid) viewers. We both enjoy Truman's inadvertent, non-consenting, exhibitionism. We know the truth about Truman and so do they. Of course, we are in a privileged moral position because we know it is a movie and they know it is a piece of raw life that they are watching.

But moviegoers throughout Hollywood's history have willingly and insatiably participated in numerous "Truman Shows". The lives (real or concocted) of the studio stars were brutally exploited and incorporated in their films. Jean Harlow, Barbara Stanwyck, James Cagney all were forced to spill their guts in cathartic acts of on camera repentance and not so symbolic humiliation. "Truman Shows" is the more common phenomenon in the movie industry.

Then there is the question of the director of the movie as God and of God as the director of a movie. The members of his team – technical and non-technical alike – obey Christoff, the director, almost blindly. They suspend their better moral judgement and succumb to his whims and to the brutal and vulgar aspects of his pervasive dishonesty and sadism. The torturer loves his victims. They define him and infuse his life with meaning. Caught in a narrative, the movie says, people act immorally.

(IN)famous psychological experiments support this assertion. Students were led to administer what they thought were "deadly" electric shocks to their colleagues or to treat them bestially in simulated prisons. They obeyed orders. So did all the hideous genocidal criminals in history. The Director Weir asks: should God be allowed to be immoral or should he be bound by morality and ethics? Should his decisions and actions be constrained by an over-riding code of right and wrong? Should we obey his commandments blindly or should we exercise judgement?

If we do exercise judgement are we then being immoral because God (and the Director Christoff) know more (about the world, about us, the viewers and about Truman), know better, are omnipotent? Is the exercise of judgement the usurpation of divine powers and attributes? Isn't this act of rebelliousness bound to lead us down the path of apocalypse?

It all boils down to the question of free choice and free will versus the benevolent determinism imposed by an omniscient and omnipotent being. What is better: to have the choice and be damned (almost inevitably, as in the biblical narrative of the Garden of Eden) – or to succumb to the superior wisdom of a supreme being? A choice always involves a dilemma. It is the conflict between two equivalent states, two weighty decisions whose outcomes are equally desirable and two identically-preferable courses of action. Where there is no such equivalence – there is no choice, merely the pre-ordained (given full knowledge) exercise of a preference or inclination. Bees do not choose to make honey. A fan of football does not choose to watch a football game. He is motivated by a clear inequity between the choices that he faces. He can read a book or go to the game. His decision is clear and pre-determined by his predilection and by the inevitable and invariable implementation of the principle of pleasure. There is no choice here. It is all rather automatic. But compare this to the choice some victims had to make between two of their children in the face of Nazi brutality. Which child to sentence to death – which one to sentence to life? Now, this is a real choice. It involves conflicting emotions of equal strength. One must not confuse decisions, opportunities and choice.

Decisions are the mere selection of courses of action. This selection can be the result of a choice or the result of a tendency (conscious, unconscious, or biological-genetic). Opportunities are current states of the world, which allow for a decision to be made and to affect the future state of the world. Choices are our conscious experience of moral or other dilemmas.

Christoff finds it strange that Truman – having discovered the truth – insists upon his right to make choices, i.e., upon his right to experience dilemmas. To the Director, dilemmas are painful, unnecessary, destructive, or at best disruptive. His utopian world – the one he constructed for Truman – is choice-free and dilemma-free. Truman is programmed not in the sense that his spontaneity is extinguished. Truman is wrong when, in one of the scenes, he keeps shouting: "Be careful, I am spontaneous". The Director and fat-cat capitalistic producers want him to be spontaneous, they want him to make decisions. But they do not want him to make choices. So they influence his preferences and predilections by providing him with an absolutely totalitarian, micro-controlled, repetitive environment. Such an environment reduces the set of possible decisions so that there is only one favourable or acceptable decision (outcome) at any junction. Truman does decide whether to walk down a certain path or not. But when he does decide to walk – only one path is available to him. His world is constrained and limited – not his actions.

Actually, Truman's only choice in the movie leads to an arguably immoral decision. He abandons ship. He walks out on the whole project. He destroys an investment of billions of dollars, people's lives and careers. He turns his back on some of the actors who seem to really be emotionally attached to him. He ignores the good and pleasure that the show has brought to the lives of millions of people (the viewers). He selfishly and vengefully goes away. He knows all this. By the time he makes his decision, he is fully informed. He knows that some people may commit suicide, go bankrupt, endure major depressive episodes, do drugs. But this massive landscape of resulting devastation does not deter him. He prefers his narrow, personal, interest. He walks.

But Truman did not ask or choose to be put in his position. He found himself responsible for all these people without being consulted. There was no consent or act of choice involved. How can anyone be responsible for the well-being and lives of other people – if he did not CHOOSE to be so responsible? Moreover, Truman had the perfect moral right to think that these people wronged him. Are we morally responsible and accountable for the well-being and lives of those who wrong us? True Christians are, for instance.

Moreover, most of us, most of the time, find ourselves in situations which we did not help mould by our decisions. We are unwillingly cast into the world. We do not provide prior consent to being born. This fundamental decision is made for us, forced upon us. This pattern persists throughout our childhood and adolescence: decisions are made elsewhere by others and influence our lives profoundly.

As adults we are the objects – often the victims – of the decisions of corrupt politicians, mad scientists, megalomaniac media barons, gung-ho generals and demented artists. This world is not of our making and our ability to shape and influence it is very limited and rather illusory. We live in our own "Truman Show". Does this mean that we are not morally responsible for others?

We are morally responsible even if we did not choose the circumstances and the parameters and characteristics of the universe that we inhabit. The Swedish Count Wallenberg imperilled his life (and lost it) smuggling hunted Jews out of Nazi occupied Europe. He did not choose, or helped to shape Nazi Europe. It was the brainchild of the deranged Director Hitler. Having found himself an unwilling participant in Hitler's horror show, Wallenberg did not turn his back and opted out. He remained within the bloody and horrific set and did his best. Truman should have done the same. Jesus said that he should have loved his enemies. He should have felt and acted with responsibility towards his fellow human beings, even towards those who wronged him greatly.

But this may be an inhuman demand. Such forgiveness and magnanimity are the reserve of God. And the fact that Truman's tormentors did not see themselves as such and believed that they were acting in his best interests and that they were catering to his every need – does not absolve them from their crimes. Truman should have maintained a fine balance between his responsibility to the show, its creators and its viewers and his natural drive to get back at his tormentors. The source of the dilemma (which led to his act of choosing) is that the two groups overlap.

Truman found himself in the impossible position of being the sole guarantor of the well-being and lives of his tormentors. To put the question in sharper relief: are we morally obliged to save the life and livelihood of someone who greatly wronged us? Or is vengeance justified in such a case?

A very problematic figure in this respect is that of Truman's best and childhood friend. They grew up together, shared secrets, emotions and adventures. Yet he lies to Truman constantly and under the Director's instructions. Everything he says is part of a script. It is this disinformation that convinces us that he is not Truman's true friend. A real friend is expected, above all, to provide us with full and true information and, thereby, to enhance our ability to choose. Truman's true love in the Show tried to do it. She paid the price: she was ousted from the show. But she tried to provide Truman with a choice. It is not sufficient to say the right things and make the right moves. Inner drive and motivation are required and the willingness to take risks (such as the risk of providing Truman with full information about his condition). All the actors who played Truman's parents, loving wife, friends and colleagues, miserably failed on this score.

It is in this mimicry that the philosophical key to the whole movie rests. A Utopia cannot be faked. Captain Nemo's utopian underwater city was a real Utopia because everyone knew everything about it. People were given a choice (though an irreversible and irrevocable one). They chose to become lifetime members of the reclusive Captain's colony and to abide by its (overly rational) rules.

The Utopia came closest to extinction when a group of stray survivors of a maritime accident were imprisoned in it against their expressed will. In the absence of choice, no utopia can exist. In the absence of full, timely and accurate information, no choice can exist. Actually, the availability of choice is so crucial that even when it is prevented by nature itself – and not by the designs of more or less sinister or monomaniac people – there can be no Utopia. In H.G. Wells' book "The Time Machine", the hero wanders off to the third millennium only to come across a peaceful Utopia. Its members are immortal, don't have to work, or think in order to survive. Sophisticated machines take care of all their needs. No one forbids them to make choices. There simply is no need to make them. So the Utopia is fake and indeed ends badly.

Finally, the "Truman Show" encapsulates the most virulent attack on capitalism in a long time. Greedy, thoughtless money machines in the form of billionaire tycoon-producers exploit Truman's life shamelessly and remorselessly in the ugliest display of human vices possible. The Director indulges in his control-mania. The producers indulge in their monetary obsession. The viewers (on both sides of the silver screen) indulge in voyeurism. The actors vie and compete in the compulsive activity of furthering their petty careers. It is a repulsive canvas of a disintegrating world. Perhaps Christoff is right after al when he warns Truman about the true nature of the world. But Truman chooses. He chooses the exit door leading to the outer darkness over the false sunlight in the Utopia that he leaves behind.

<u>Return</u>

The Matrix

It is easy to confuse the concepts of "virtual reality" and a "computerized model of reality (simulation)". The former is a self-contained Universe, replete with its "laws of physics" and "logic". It can bear resemblance to the real world or not. It can be consistent or not. It can interact with the real world or not. In short, it is an arbitrary environment. In contrast, a model of reality must have a direct and strong relationship to the world. It must obey the rules of physics and of logic. The absence of such a relationship renders it meaningless. A flight simulator is not much good in a world without aeroplanes or if it ignores the laws of nature. A technical analysis program is useless without a stock exchange or if its mathematically erroneous.

Yet, the two concepts are often confused because they are both mediated by and reside on computers. The computer is a self-contained (though not closed) Universe. It incorporates the hardware, the data and the instructions for the manipulation of the data (software). It is, therefore, by definition, a virtual reality. It is versatile and can correlate its reality with the world outside. But it can also refrain from doing so. This is the ominous "what if" in artificial intelligence (AI). What if a computer were to refuse to correlate its internal (virtual) reality with the reality of its makers? What if it were to impose its own reality on us and make it the privileged one?

In the visually tantalizing movie, "The Matrix", a breed of AI computers takes over the world. It harvests human embryos in laboratories called "fields". It then feeds them through grim looking tubes and keeps them immersed in gelatinous liquid in cocoons. This new "machine species" derives its energy needs from the electricity produced by the billions of human bodies thus preserved. A sophisticated, all-pervasive, computer program called "The Matrix" generates a "world" inhabited by the consciousness of the unfortunate human batteries. Ensconced in their shells, they see themselves walking, talking, working and making love. This is a tangible and olfactory phantasm masterfully created by the Matrix. Its computing power is mind boggling. It generates the minutest details and reams of data in a spectacularly successful effort to maintain the illusion.

A group of human miscreants succeeds to learn the secret of the Matrix. They form an underground and live aboard a ship, loosely communicating with a halcyon city called "Zion", the last bastion of resistance. In one of the scenes, Cypher, one of the rebels defects. Over a glass of (illusory) rubicund wine and (spectral) juicy steak, he poses the main dilemma of the movie. Is it better to live happily in a perfectly detailed delusion - or to survive unhappily but free of its hold?

The Matrix controls the minds of all the humans in the world. It is a bridge between them, they inter-connected through it. It makes them share the same sights, smells and textures. They remember. They compete. They make decisions.

The Matrix is sufficiently complex to allow for this apparent lack of determinism and ubiquity of free will. The root question is: is there any difference between making decisions and feeling certain of making them (not having made them)? If one is unaware of the existence of the Matrix, the answer is no. From the inside, as a part of the Matrix, making decisions and appearing to be making them are identical states. Only an outside observer - one who in possession of full information regarding both the Matrix and the humans - can tell the difference.

Moreover, if the Matrix were a computer program of infinite complexity, no observer (finite or infinite) would have been able to say with any certainty whose a decision was - the Matrix's or the human's. And because the Matrix, for all intents and purposes, is infinite compared to the mind of any single, tube-nourished, individual - it is safe to say that the states of "making a decision" and "appearing to be making a decision" are subjectively indistinguishable. No individual within the Matrix would be able to tell the difference. His or her life would seem to him or her as real as ours are to us. The Matrix may be deterministic - but this determinism is inaccessible to individual minds because of the complexity involved. When faced with a trillion deterministic paths, one would be justified to feel that he exercised free, unconstrained will in choosing one of them. Free will and determinism are indistinguishable at a certain level of complexity.

Yet, we KNOW that the Matrix is different to our world. It is NOT the same. This is an intuitive kind of knowledge, for sure, but this does not detract from its firmness. If there is no subjective difference between the Matrix and our Universe, there must be an objective one. Another key sentence is uttered by Morpheus, the leader of the rebels. He says to "The Chosen One" (the Messiah) that it is really the year 2199, though the Matrix gives the impression that it is 1999.

This is where the Matrix and reality diverge. Though a human who would experience both would find them indistinguishable - objectively they are different. In one of them (the Matrix), people have no objective TIME (though the Matrix might have it). The other (reality) is governed by it.

Under the spell of the Matrix, people feel as though time goes by. They have functioning watches. The sun rises and sets. Seasons change. They grow old and die. This is not entirely an illusion. Their bodies do decay and die, as ours do. They are not exempt from the laws of nature. But their AWARENESS of time is computer generated. The Matrix is sufficiently sophisticated and knowledgeable to maintain a close correlation between the physical state of the human (his health and age) and his consciousness of the passage of time. The basic rules of time - for instance, its asymmetry - are part of the program.

But this is precisely it. Time in the minds of these people is program-generated, not reality-induced. It is not the derivative of change and irreversible (thermodynamic and other) processes OUT THERE. Their minds are part of a computer program and the computer program is a part of their minds.

Their bodies are static, degenerating in their protective nests. Nothing happens to them except in their minds. They have no physical effect on the world. They effect no change. These things set the Matrix and reality apart.

To "qualify" as reality a two-way interaction must occur. One flow of data is when reality influences the minds of people (as does the Matrix). The obverse, but equally necessary, type of data flow is when people know reality and influence it. The Matrix triggers a time sensation in people the same way that the Universe triggers a time sensation in us. Something does happen OUT THERE and it is called the Matrix. In this sense, the Matrix is real, it is the reality of these humans. It maintains the requirement of the first type of flow of data. But it fails the second test: people do not know that it exists or any of its attributes, nor do they affect it irreversibly. They do not change the Matrix. Paradoxically, the rebels do affect the Matrix (they almost destroy it). In doing so, they make it REAL. It is their REALITY because they KNOW it and they irreversibly CHANGE it.

Applying this dual-track test, "virtual" reality IS a reality, albeit, at this stage, of a deterministic type. It affects our minds, we know that it exists and we affect it in return. Our choices and actions irreversibly alter the state of the system. This altered state, in turn, affects our minds. This interaction IS what we call "reality". With the advent of stochastic and quantum virtual reality generators - the distinction between "real" and "virtual" will fade. The Matrix thus is not impossible. But that it is possible - does not make it real.

Appendix - God and Gödel

The second movie in the Matrix series - "The Matrix Reloaded" - culminates in an encounter between Neo ("The One") and the architect of the Matrix (a thinly disguised God, white beard and all). The architect informs Neo that he is the sixth reincarnation of The One and that Zion, a shelter for those decoupled from the Matrix, has been destroyed before and is about to be demolished again.

The architect goes on to reveal that his attempts to render the Matrix "harmonious" (perfect) failed. He was, thus, forced to introduce an element of intuition into the equations to reflect the unpredictability and "grotesqueries" of human nature. This in-built error tends to accumulate over time and to threaten the very existence of the Matrix - hence the need to obliterate Zion, the seat of malcontents and rebels, periodically.

God appears to be unaware of the work of an important, though eccentric, Czech-Austrian mathematical logician, Kurt Gödel (1906-1978). A passing acquaintance with his two theorems would have saved the architect a lot of time.

Gödel's First Incompleteness Theorem states that every consistent axiomatic logical system, sufficient to express arithmetic, contains true but unprovable ("not decidable") sentences. In certain cases (when the system is omega-consistent), both said sentences and their negation are unprovable. The system is consistent and true - but not "complete" because not all its sentences can be decided as true or false by either being proved or by being refuted.

The Second Incompleteness Theorem is even more earth-shattering. It says that no consistent formal logical system can prove its own consistency. The system may be complete - but then we are unable to show, using its axioms and inference laws, that it is consistent

In other words, a computational system, like the Matrix, can either be complete and inconsistent - or consistent and incomplete. By trying to construct a system both complete and consistent, God has run afoul of Gödel's theorem and made possible the third sequel, "Matrix Revolutions".

Return

The Shattered Identity

Read these essays first:

The Habitual Identity

Death, Meaning, and Identity

Fact and Truth

Dreams - The Metaphors of Mind

I. Exposition

In the movie "Shattered" (1991), Dan Merrick survives an accident and develops total amnesia regarding his past. His battered face is reconstructed by plastic surgeons and, with the help of his loving wife, he gradually recovers his will to live. But he never develops a proper sense of identity. It is as though he is constantly ill at ease in his own body. As the plot unravels, Dan is led to believe that he may have murdered his wife's lover, Jack. This thriller offers additional twists and turns but, throughout it all, we face this question:

Dan has no recollection of being Dan. Dan does not remember murdering Jack. It seems as though Dan's very identity has been erased. Yet, Dan is in sound mind and can tell right from wrong. Should Dan be held (morally and, as a result, perhaps legally as well) accountable for Jack's murder?

Would the answer to this question still be the same had Dan erased from his memory ONLY the crime -but recalled everything else (in an act of selective dissociation)? Do our moral and legal accountability and responsibility spring from the integrity of our memories? If Dan were to be punished for a crime he doesn't have the faintest recollection of committing - wouldn't he feel horribly wronged? Wouldn't he be justified in feeling so?

There are many states of consciousness that involve dissociation and selective amnesia: hypnosis, trance and possession, hallucination, illusion, memory disorders (like organic, or functional amnesia), depersonalization disorder, dissociative fugue, dreaming, psychosis, post traumatic stress disorder, and drug-induced psychotomimetic states.

Consider this, for instance:

What if Dan were the victim of a Multiple Personality Disorder (now known as "Dissociative Identity Disorder")? What if one of his "alters" (i.e., one of the multitude of "identities" sharing Dan's mind and body) committed the crime? Should Dan still be held responsible? What if the alter "John" committed the crime and then "vanished", leaving behind another alter (let us say, "Joseph") in control?

Should "Joseph" be held responsible for the crime "John" committed? What if "John" were to reappear 10 years after he "vanished"? What if he were to reappear 50 years after he "vanished"? What if he were to reappear for a period of 90 days - only to "vanish" again? And what is Dan's role in all this? Who, exactly, then, is Dan?

II. Who is Dan?

Buddhism compares Man to a river. Both retain their identity despite the fact that their individual composition is different at different moments. The possession of a body as the foundation of a self-identity is a dubious proposition. Bodies change drastically in time (consider a baby compared to an adult). Almost all the cells in a human body are replaced every few years. Changing one's brain (by transplantation) - also changes one's identity, even if the rest of the body remains the same.

Thus, the only thing that binds a "person" together (i.e., gives him a self and an identity) is time, or, more precisely, memory. By "memory" I also mean: personality, skills, habits, retrospected emotions - in short: all long term imprints and behavioural patterns. The body is not an accidental and insignificant container, of course. It constitutes an important part of one's self-image, self-esteem, sense of self-worth, and sense of existence (spatial, temporal, and social). But one can easily imagine a brain in vitro as having the same identity as when it resided in a body. One cannot imagine a body without a brain (or with a different brain) as having the same identity it had before the brain was removed or replaced.

What if the brain in vitro (in the above example) could not communicate with us at all? Would we still think it is possessed of a self? The biological functions of people in coma are maintained. But do they have an identity, a self? If yes, why do we "pull the plug" on them so often?

It would seem (as it did to Locke) that we accept that someone has a self-identity if: (a) He has the same hardware as we do (notably, a brain) and (b) He communicates his humanly recognizable and comprehensible inner world to us and manipulates his environment. We accept that he has a given (i.e., the same continuous) self-identity if (c) He shows consistent intentional (i.e., willed) patterns ("memory") in doing (b) for a long period of time.

It seems that we accept that we have a self-identity (i.e., we are self-conscious) if (a) We discern (usually through introspection) long term consistent intentional (i.e., willed) patterns ("memory") in our manipulation ("relating to") of our environment and (b) Others accept that we have a self-identity (Herbert Mead, Feuerbach).

Dan (probably) has the same hardware as we do (a brain). He communicates his (humanly recognizable and comprehensible) inner world to us (which is how he manipulates us and his environment). Thus, Dan clearly has a self-identity. But he is inconsistent. His intentional (willed) patterns, his memory, are incompatible with those demonstrated by Dan before the accident. Though he clearly is possessed of a self-identity, we cannot say that he has the SAME self-identity he possessed before the crash. In other words, we cannot say that he, indeed, is Dan.

Dan himself does not feel that he has a self-identity at all. He discerns intentional (willed) patterns in his manipulation of his environment but, due to his amnesia, he cannot tell if these are consistent, or long term. In other words, Dan has no memory. Moreover, others do not accept him as Dan (or have their doubts) because they have no memory of Dan as he is now.

Interim conclusion:

Having a memory is a necessary and sufficient condition for possessing a self-identity.

III. Repression

Yet, resorting to memory to define identity may appear to be a circular (even tautological) argument. When we postulate memory - don't we already presuppose the existence of a "remembering agent" with an established self-identity?

Moreover, we keep talking about "discerning", "intentional", or "willed" patterns. But isn't a big part of our self (in the form of the unconscious, full of repressed memories) unavailable to us? Don't we develop defence mechanisms against repressed memories and fantasies, against unconscious content incongruent with our self-image? Even worse, this hidden, inaccessible, dynamically active part of our self is thought responsible for our recurrent discernible patterns of behaviour. The phenomenon of posthypnotic suggestion seems to indicate that this may be the case. The existence of a self-identity is, therefore, determined through introspection (by oneself) and observation (by others) of merely the conscious part of the self.

But the unconscious is as much a part of one's self-identity as one's conscious. What if, due to a mishap, the roles were reversed? What if Dan's conscious part were to become his unconscious and his unconscious part - his conscious? What if all his conscious memories, drives, fears, wishes, fantasies, and hopes - were to become unconscious while his repressed memories, drives, etc. - were to become conscious? Would we still say that it is "the same" Dan and that he retains his self-identity? Not very likely. And yet, one's (unremembered) unconscious - for instance, the conflict between id and ego - determines one's personality and self-identity.

The main contribution of psychoanalysis and later psychodynamic schools is the understanding that self-identity is a dynamic, evolving, ever-changing construct - and not a static, inertial, and passive entity. It casts doubt over the meaningfulness of the question with which we ended the exposition: "Who, exactly, then, is Dan?" Dan is different at different stages of his life (Erikson) and he constantly evolves in accordance with his innate nature (Jung), past history (Adler), drives (Freud), cultural milieu (Horney), upbringing (Klein, Winnicott), needs (Murray), or the interplay with his genetic makeup. Dan is not a thing - he is a process. Even Dan's personality traits and cognitive style, which may well be stable, are often influenced by Dan's social setting and by his social interactions.

It would seem that having a memory is a necessary but insufficient condition for possessing a self-identity. One cannot remember one's unconscious states (though one can remember their outcomes). One often forgets events, names, and other information even if it was conscious at a given time in one's past. Yet, one's (unremembered) unconscious is an integral and important part of one's identity and one's self. The remembered as well as the unremembered constitute one's self-identity.

IV. *The Memory Link*

Hume said that to be considered in possession of a mind, a creature needs to have a few states of consciousness linked by memory in a kind of narrative or personal mythology. Can this conjecture be equally applied to unconscious mental states (e.g. subliminal perceptions, beliefs, drives, emotions, desires, etc.)?

In other words, can we rephrase Hume and say that to be considered in possession of a mind, a creature needs to have a few states of consciousness and a few states of the unconscious - all linked by memory into a personal narrative? Isn't it a contradiction in terms to remember the unconscious?

The unconscious and the subliminal are instance of the general category of mental phenomena which are not states of consciousness (i.e., are not conscious). Sleep and hypnosis are two others. But so are "background mental phenomena" - e.g., one holds onto one's beliefs and knowledge even when one is not aware (conscious) of them at every given moment.

We know that an apple will fall towards the earth, we know how to drive a car ("automatically"), and we believe that the sun will rise tomorrow, even though we do not spend every second of our waking life consciously thinking about falling apples, driving cars, or the position of the sun.

Yet, the fact that knowledge and beliefs and other background mental phenomena are not constantly conscious - does not mean that they cannot be remembered. They can be remembered either by an act of will, or in (sometimes an involuntary) response to changes in the environment. The same applies to all other unconscious content. Unconscious content can be recalled. Psychoanalysis, for instance, is about re-introducing repressed unconscious content to the patient's conscious memory and thus making it "remembered".

In fact, one's self-identity may be such a background mental phenomenon (always there, not always conscious, not always remembered). The acts of will which bring it to the surface are what we call "memory" and "introspection".

This would seem to imply that having a self-identity is independent of having a memory (or the ability to introspect). Memory is just the mechanism by which one becomes aware of one's background, "always-on", and omnipresent (all-pervasive) self-identity. Self-identity is the object and predicate of memory and introspection. It is as though self-identity were an emergent extensive parameter of the complex human system - measurable by the dual techniques of memory and introspection.

We, therefore, have to modify our previous conclusions:

Having a memory is not a necessary nor a sufficient condition for possessing a self-identity.

We are back to square one. The poor souls in Oliver Sacks' tome, "The Man Who Mistook his Wife for a Hat" are unable to create and retain memories. They occupy an eternal present, with no past. They are thus unable to access (or invoke) their self-identity by remembering it. Their self-identity is unavailable to them (though it is available to those who observe them over many years) - but it exists for sure. Therapy often succeeds in restoring pre-amnesiac memories and self-identity.

V. The Incorrigible Self

Self-identity is not only always-on and all-pervasive - but also incorrigible. In other words, no one - neither an observer, nor the person himself - can "disprove" the existence of his self-identity. No one can prove that a report about the existence of his (or another's) self-identity is mistaken.

Is it equally safe to say that no one - neither an observer, nor the person himself - can prove (or disprove) the non-existence of his self-identity? Would it be correct to say that no one can prove that a report about the non-existence of his (or another's) self-identity is true or false?

Dan's criminal responsibility crucially depends on the answers to these questions. Dan cannot be held responsible for Jack's murder if he can prove that he is ignorant of the facts of his action (i.e., if he can prove the non-existence of his self-identity). If he has no access to his (former) self-identity - he can hardly be expected to be aware and cognizant of these facts.

What is in question is not Dan's mens rea, nor the application of the McNaghten tests (did Dan know the nature and quality of his act or could he tell right from wrong) to determine whether Dan was insane when he committed the crime. A much broader issue is at stake: is it the same person? Is the murderous Dan the same person as the current Dan? Even though Dan seems to own the same body and brain and is manifestly sane - he patently has no access to his (former) self-identity. He has changed so drastically that it is arguable whether he is still the same person - he has been "replaced".

Finally, we can try to unite all the strands of our discourse into this double definition:

It would seem that we accept that someone has a self-identity if: (a) He has the same hardware as we do (notably, a brain) and, by implication, the same software as we do (an all-pervasive, omnipresent self-identity) and (b) He communicates his humanly recognizable and comprehensible inner world to us and manipulates his environment. We accept that he has a specific (i.e., the same continuous) self-identity if (c) He shows consistent intentional (i.e., willed) patterns ("memory") in doing (b) for a long period of time.

It seems that we accept that we have a specific self-identity (i.e., we are self-conscious of a specific identity) if (a) We discern (usually through memory and introspection) long term consistent intentional (i.e., willed) patterns ("memory") in our manipulation ("relating to") of our environment and (b) Others accept that we have a specific self-identity.

In conclusion: Dan undoubtedly has a self-identity (being human and, thus, endowed with a brain). Equally undoubtedly, this self-identity is not Dan's (but a new, unfamiliar, one).

Such is the stuff of our nightmares - body snatching, demonic possession, waking up in a strange place, not knowing who we are. Without a continuous personal history - we are not. It is what binds our various bodies, states of mind, memories, skills, emotions, and cognitions - into a coherent bundle of identity. Dan speaks, drinks, dances, talks, and makes love - but throughout that time, he is not present because he does not remember Dan and how it is to be Dan. He may have murdered Jake - but, by all philosophical and ethical criteria, it was most definitely not his fault.

Return

Titanic, or a Moral Deliberation

The film "Titanic" is riddled with moral dilemmas. In one of the scenes, the owner of Star Line, the shipping company that owned the now-sinking Unsinkable, joins a lowered life-boat. The tortured expression on his face demonstrates that even he experiences more than unease at his own conduct. Prior to the disaster, he instructs the captain to adopt a policy dangerous to the ship. Indeed, it proves fatal. A complicating factor was the fact that only women and children were allowed by the officers in charge into the lifeboats. Another was the discrimination against Third Class passengers. The boats sufficed only to half the number of those on board and the First Class, High Society passengers were preferred over the Low-Life immigrants under deck.

Why do we all feel that the owner should have stayed on and faced his inevitable death? Because we judge him responsible for the demise of the ship. Additionally, his wrong instructions – motivated by greed and the pursuit of celebrity – were a crucial contributing factor. The owner should have been punished (in his future) for things that he has done (in his past). This is intuitively appealing.

Would we have rendered the same judgement had the Titanic's fate been the outcome of accident and accident alone? If the owner of the ship could have had no control over the circumstances of its horrible ending – would we have still condemned him for saving his life? Less severely, perhaps. So, the fact that a moral entity has ACTED (or omitted, or refrained from acting) in its past is essential in dispensing with future rewards or punishments.

The "product liability" approach also fits here. The owner (and his "long arms": manufacturer, engineers, builders, etc.) of the Titanic were deemed responsible because they implicitly contracted with their passengers. They made a representation (which was explicit in their case but is implicit in most others): "This ship was constructed with knowledge and forethought. The best design was employed to avoid danger. The best materials to increase pleasure." That the Titanic sank was an irreversible breach of this contract. In a way, it was an act of abrogation of duties and obligations. The owner/manufacturer of a product must compensate the consumers should his product harm them in any manner that they were not explicitly, clearly, visibly and repeatedly warned against. Moreover, he should even make amends if the product failed to meet the reasonable and justified expectations of consumers, based on such warrants and representations. The payment should be either in kind (as in more ancient justice systems) or in cash (as in modern Western civilization).

The product called "Titanic" took away the lives of its end-users. Our "gut justice" tells us that the owner should have paid in kind. Faulty engineering, insufficient number of lifeboats, over-capacity, hubris, passengers and crew not drilled to face emergencies, extravagant claims regarding the ship's resilience, contravening the captain's professional judgement. All these seem to be sufficient grounds to the death penalty.

And yet, this is not the real question. The serious problem is this : WHY should anyone pay in his future for his actions in the past? First, there are some thorny issues to be eliminated. Such as determinism: if there is no free will, there can be no personal responsibility. Another is the preservation of personal identity: are the person who committed the act and the person who is made to pay for it – one and the same? If the answer is in the affirmative, in which sense are they the same, the physical, the mental? Is the "overlap" only limited and probabilistic? Still, we could assume, for this discussion's sake, that the personal identity is undeniably and absolutely preserved and that there is free will and, therefore, that people can predict the outcomes of their actions, to a reasonable degree of accuracy and that they elect to accept these outcomes prior to the commission of their acts or to their omission. All this does not answer the question that opened this paragraph. Even if there were a contract signed between the acting person and the world, in which the person willingly, consciously and intelligently (=without diminished responsibility) accepted the future outcome of his acts, the questions would remain: WHY should it be so? Why cannot we conceive of a world in which acts and outcomes are divorced? It is because we cannot believe in an a-causal world.

Causality is a relationship (mostly between two things, or, rather, events, the cause and the effect). Something generates or produces another. Therefore, it is the other's efficient cause and it acts upon it (=it acts to bring it about) through the mechanism of efficient causation. A cause can be a direct physical mechanism or an explanatory feature (historical cause). Of Aristotle's Four Causes (Formal, Material, Efficient and Final), only the efficient cause creates something distinguishable from itself. The causal discourse, therefore, is problematic (how can a cause lead to an effect, indistinguishable from itself?). Singular Paradigmatic Causal Statements (Event A caused Event B) differ from General ones (Event A causes Event B). Both are inadequate in dealing with mundane, routine, causal statements because they do not reveal an OVERT relation between the two events discussed. Moreover, in daily usage we treat facts (as well as events) as causes. Not all the philosophers are in agreement regarding factual causation. Davidson, for instance, admits that facts can be RELEVANT to causal explanations but refuses to accept them AS reasons. Acts may be distinct from facts, philosophically, but not in day-to-day regular usage. By laymen (the vast majority of humanity, that is), though, they are perceived to be the same.

Pairs of events that are each other's cause and effect are accorded a special status. But, that one follows the other (even if invariably) is insufficient grounds to endow them with this status. This is the famous "Post hoc, ergo propter hoc" fallacy. Other relations must be weighed and the possibility of common causation must be seriously contemplated. Such sequencing is, conceptually, not even necessary: simultaneous causation and backwards causation are part of modern physics, for instance.

Time seems to be irrelevant to the status of events, though both time and causation share an asymmetric structure (A causes B but B does not cause A). The direction (the asymmetry) of the causal chain is not of the same type as the direction (asymmetry) of time. The former is formal, the latter, presumably, physical, or mental. A more serious problem, to my mind, is the converse: what sets apart causal (cause and effect) pairs of events from other pairs in which both member-events are the outcomes of a common cause? Event B can invariably follow Event A and still not be its effect. Both events could have been caused by a common cause. A cause either necessitates the effect, or is a sufficient condition for its occurrence. The sequence is either inevitable, or possible. The meaninglessness of this sentence is evident.

Here, philosophers diverge. Some say (following Hume's reasoning and his constant conjunction relation between events) that a necessary causal relation exists between events when one is the inevitable outcome (=follows) the other. Others propound a weaker version: the necessity of the effect is hypothetical or conditional, given the laws of nature. Put differently: to say that A necessitates (=causes) B is no more than to say that it is a result of the laws of nature that when A happens, so does B. Hempel generalized this approach. He said that a statement of a fact (whether a private or a general fact) is explained only if deduced from other statements, at least one of which is a statement of a general scientific law.

This is the "Covering Law Model" and it implies a symmetry between explaining and predicting (at least where private facts are concerned). If an event can be explained, it could have been predicted and vice versa. Needless to say that Hempel's approach did not get us nearer to solving the problems of causal priority and of indeterministic causation.

The Empiricists went a step further. They stipulated that the laws of nature are contingencies and not necessary truths. Other chains of events are possible where the laws of nature are different. This is the same tired regularity theory in a more exotic guise. They are all descendants of Hume's definition of causality: "An object followed by another and where all the objects that resemble the first are followed by objects that resemble the second." Nothing in the world is, therefore, a causal necessity, events are only constantly conjoined. Regularities in our experience condition us to form the idea of causal necessity and to deduce that causes must generate events. Kant called this latter deduction "A bastard of the imagination, impregnated by experience" with no legitimate application in the world. It also constituted a theological impediment. God is considered to be "Causa Sui", His own cause. But any application of a causal chain or force, already assumes the existence of a cause. This existence cannot, therefore, be the outcome of the use made of it. God had to be recast as the uncaused cause of the existence of all things contingent and His existence necessitated no cause because He, himself, is necessary. This is flimsy stuff and it gets even flimsier when the issue of causal deviance is debated.

A causal deviance is an abnormal, though causal, relation between events or states of the world. It mainly arises when we introduce intentional action and perception into the theory of causation. Let us revert to the much-maligned owner of the sinking Titanic. He intended to do one thing and another happened. Granted, if he intended to do something and his intention was the cause of his doing so – then we could have said that he intentionally committed an act. But what if he intended to do one thing and out came another? And what if he intended to do something, mistakenly did something else and, still, accidentally, achieved what he set out to do? The popular example is if someone intends to do something and gets so nervous that it happens even without an act being committed (intends to refuse an invitation by his boss, gets so nervous that he falls asleep and misses the party). Are these actions and intentions in their classical senses? There is room for doubt. Davidson narrows down the demands. To him, "thinking causes" (causally efficient propositional attitudes) are nothing but causal relations between events with the right application of mental predicates which ascribe propositional attitudes supervening the right application of physical predicates. This approach omits intention altogether, not to mention the ascription of desire and belief.

But shouldn't have the hapless owner availed his precious place to women and children? Should not he have obeyed the captain's orders (=the marine law)? Should we succumb to laws that put our lives at risk (fight in a war, sink with a ship)? The reason that women and children are preferred over men is that they represent the future. They are either capable of bringing life to the world (women) – or of living longer (children). Societal etiquette reflects the arithmetic of the species, in this (and in many another) case. But if this were entirely and exclusively so, then young girls and female infants would have been preferred over all the other groups of passengers. Old women would have been left with the men, to die. That the actual (and declared) selection processes differed from our theoretical exercise says a lot about the vigorousness and applicability of our theories – and a lot about the real world out there. The owner's behaviour may have been deplorable – but it, definitely, was natural. He put his interests (his survival) above the concerns of his society and his species. Most of us would have done the same under the same circumstances.

The owner of the ship – though "Newly Rich" – undoubtedly belonged to the First Class, Upper Crust, Cream of Society passengers. These were treated to the lifeboats before the passengers of the lower classes and decks. Was this a morally right decision? For sure, it was not politically correct, in today's terms. Class and money distinctions were formally abolished three decades ago in the enlightened West. Discrimination between human beings in now allowed only on the basis of merit (=on the basis of one's natural endowments). Why should we think one basis for discrimination preferable to another? Can we eliminate discrimination completely and if it were possible, would it have been desirable?

The answers, in my view, are that no basis of discrimination can hold the moral high ground. They are all morally problematic because they are deterministic and assign independent, objective, exogenous values to humans. On the other hand, we are not born equal, nor do we proceed to develop equally, or live under the same circumstances and conditions. It is impossible to equate the unequal. Discrimination is not imposed by humans on an otherwise egalitarian world. It is introduced by the world into human society. And the elimination of discrimination would constitute a grave error. The inequalities among humans and the ensuing conflicts are the fuel that feeds the engines of human development. Hopes, desires, aspirations and inspiration are all the derivatives of discrimination or of the wish to be favoured, or preferred over others. Disparities of money create markets, labour, property, planning, wealth and capital. Mental inequalities lead to innovation and theory. Knowledge differentials are at the heart of educational institutions, professionalism, government and so on. Osmotic and diffusive forces in human society are all the results of incongruences, disparities, differences, inequalities and the negative and positive emotions attached to them. The passengers of the first class were preferred because they paid more for their tickets. Inevitably, a tacit portion of the price went to amortize the costs of "class insurance": should anything bad happen to this boat, persons who paid a superior price will be entitled to receive a superior treatment. There is nothing morally wrong with this. Some people get to sit in the front rows of a theatre, or to travel in luxury, or to receive superior medical treatment (or any medical treatment) precisely because of this reason. There is no practical or philosophical difference between an expensive liver transplant and a place in a life boat. Both are lifesavers.

A natural disaster is no Great Equalizer. Nothing is. Even the argument that money is "external" or "accidental" to the rich individual is weak. Often, people who marry for money considerations are judged to be insincere or worse (cunning, conspiring, evil). "He married her for her money", we say, as though the she-owner and the money were two separate things. The equivalent sentence: "He married her for her youth or for her beauty" sounds flawed. But youth and beauty are more temporary and transient than money. They are really accidental because the individual has no responsibility for or share in their generation and has no possibility to effect their long-term preservation. Money, on the other hand, is generated or preserved (or both) owing to the personality of its owner. It is a better reflection of personality than youth, beauty and many other (transient or situation-dependent) "character" traits. Money is an integral part of its owner and a reliable witness as to his mental disposition. It is, therefore, a valid criterion for discrimination.

The other argument in favour of favouring the first class passengers is their contribution to society. A rich person contributes more to his society in the shorter and medium term than a poor person. Vincent Van Gogh may have been a million times more valuable to humanity, as a whole, than his brother Theo – in the long run. But in the intermediate term, Theo made it possible for Vincent and many others (family, employees, suppliers, their dependants and his country) to survive by virtue of his wealth. Rich people feed and cloth poor people directly (employment, donations) and indirectly (taxation). The opposite, alas, is not the case. Yet, this argument is flawed because it does not take time into account. We have no way to predict the future with any certainty.

Each person carries the Marshall's baton in his bag, the painter's brush, the author's fables. It is the potential that should count. A selection process, which would have preferred Theo to Vincent would have been erroneous. In the long run, Vincent proved more beneficial to human society and in more ways – including financially – then Theo could have ever been.

Return

Being John Malkovich

A quintessential loser, an out-of-job puppeteer, is hired by a firm, whose offices are ensconced in a half floor (literally. The ceiling is about a metre high, reminiscent of Taniel's hallucinatory Alice in Wonderland illustrations). By sheer accident, he discovers a tunnel (a "portal", in Internet-age parlance), which sucks its visitors into the mind of the celebrated actor, John Malkovich. The movie is a tongue in cheek discourse of identity, gender and passion in an age of languid promiscuity. It poses all the right metaphysical riddles and presses the viewers' intellectual stimulation buttons.

A two line bit of dialogue, though, forms the axis of this nightmarishly chimerical film. John Malkovich (played by himself), enraged and bewildered by the unabashed commercial exploitation of the serendipitous portal to his mind, insists that Craig, the aforementioned puppet master, cease and desist with his activities. "It is MY brain" - he screams and, with a typical American finale, "I will see you in court". Craig responds: "But, it was I who discovered the portal. It is my livelihood".

This apparently innocuous exchange disguises a few very unsettling ethical dilemmas.

The basic question is "whose brain is it, anyway"? Does John Malkovich OWN his brain? Is one's brain - one's PROPERTY? Property is usually acquired somehow. Is our brain "acquired"? It is clear that we do not acquire the hardware (neurones) and software (electrical and chemical pathways) we are born with. But it is equally clear that we do "acquire" both brain mass and the contents of our brains (its wiring or irreversible chemical changes) through learning and experience. Does this process of acquisition endow us with property rights?

It would seem that property rights pertaining to human bodies are fairly restricted. We have no right to sell our kidneys, for instance. Or to destroy our body through the use of drugs. Or to commit an abortion at will. Yet, the law does recognize and strives to enforce copyrights, patents and other forms of intellectual property rights.

This dichotomy is curious. For what is intellectual property but a mere record of the brain's activities? A book, a painting, an invention are the documentation and representation of brain waves. They are mere shadows, symbols of the real presence - our mind. How can we reconcile this contradiction? We are deemed by the law to be capable of holding full and unmitigated rights to the PRODUCTS of our brain activity, to the recording and documentation of our brain waves. But we hold only partial rights to the brain itself, their originator.

This can be somewhat understood if we were to consider this article, for instance. It is composed on a word processor. I do not own full rights to the word processing software (merely a licence), nor is the laptop I use my property - but I posses and can exercise and enforce full rights regarding this article.

Admittedly, it is a partial parallel, at best: the computer and word processing software are passive elements. It is my brain that does the authoring. And so, the mystery remains: how can I own the article - but not my brain? Why do I have the right to ruin the article at will - but not to annihilate my brain at whim?

Another angle of philosophical attack is to say that we rarely hold rights to nature or to life. We can copyright a photograph we take of a forest - but not the forest. To reduce it to the absurd: we can own a sunset captured on film - but never the phenomenon thus documented. The brain is natural and life's pivot - could this be why we cannot fully own it?

Wrong premises inevitably lead to wrong conclusions. We often own natural objects and manifestations, including those related to human life directly. We even issue patents for sequences of human DNA. And people do own forests and rivers and the specific views of sunsets.

Some scholars raise the issues of exclusivity and scarcity as the precursors of property rights. My brain can be accessed only by myself and its is one of a kind (sui generis). True but not relevant. One cannot rigorously derive from these properties of our brain a right to deny others access to them (should this become technologically feasible) - or even to set a price on such granted access. In other words, exclusivity and scarcity do not constitute property rights or even lead to their establishment. Other rights may be at play (the right to privacy, for instance) - but not the right to own property and to derive economic benefits from such ownership.

On the contrary, it is surprisingly easy to think of numerous exceptions to a purported natural right of single access to one's brain. If one memorized the formula to cure AIDS or cancer and refused to divulge it for a reasonable compensation - surely, we should feel entitled to invade his brain and extract it? Once such technology is available - shouldn't authorized bodies of inspection have access to the brains of our leaders on a periodic basis? And shouldn't we all gain visitation rights to the minds of great men and women of science, art and culture - as we do today gain access to their homes and to the products of their brains?

There is one hidden assumption, though, in both the movie and this article. It is that mind and brain are one. The portal leads to John Malkovich's MIND - yet, he keeps talking about his BRAIN and writhing physically on the screen. The portal is useless without JM's mind. Indeed, one can wonder whether JM's mind is not an INTEGRAL part of the portal - structurally and functionally inseparable from it. If so, does not the discoverer of the portal hold equal rights to John Malkovich's mind, an integral part thereof?

The portal leads to JM's mind. Can we prove that it leads to his brain? Is this identity automatic? Of course not. It is the old psychophysical question, at the heart of dualism - still far from resolved. Can a MIND be copyrighted or patented? If no one knows WHAT is the mind - how can it be the subject of laws and rights? If JM is bothered by the portal voyagers, the intruders - he surely has legal recourse, but not through the application of the rights to own property and to benefit from it. These rights provide him with no remedy because their subject (the mind) is a mystery.

Can JM sue Craig and his clientele for unauthorized visits to his mind (trespassing) - IF he is unaware of their comings and goings and unperturbed by them? Moreover, can he prove that the portal leads to HIS mind, that it is HIS mind that is being visited? Is there a way to PROVE that one has visited another's mind? (See: "On Empathy").

And if property rights to one's brain and mind were firmly established - how will telepathy (if ever proven) be treated legally? Or mind reading? The recording of dreams? Will a distinction be made between a mere visit - and the exercise of influence on the host and his / her manipulation (similar questions arise in time travel)?

This, precisely, is where the film crosses the line between the intriguing and the macabre. The master puppeteer, unable to resist his urges, manipulates John Malkovich and finally possesses him completely. This is so clearly wrong, so manifestly forbidden, so patently immoral, that the film loses its urgent ambivalence, its surrealistic moral landscape and deteriorates into another banal comedy of situations.

Return

Dreamcatcher: The Myth of Destructibility

Read these essays first:

The Habitual Identity

Death, Meaning, and Identity

In the movie "Dreamcatcher", four childhood friends, exposed to an alien, disguised as a retarded child, develop psychic powers. Years later they reunite only to confront a vicious extraterrestrial life-form. Only two survive but they succeed to eradicate the monster by incinerating it and crushing its tiny off-spring underfoot.

Being mortal ourselves, we cannot conceive of an indestructible entity. The artifacts of popular culture - thrillers, action and sci-fi films, video games, computer viruses - assume that all organisms, organizations and automata possess fatal vulnerabilities. Medicine and warfare are predicated on a similar contention.

We react with shock and horror when we are faced with "resistant stains" of bacteria or with creatures, machines, or groups able to survive and thrive in extremely hostile environments.

Destruction is multi-faceted. Even the simplest system has a structure and performs functions. If the spatial continuity or arrangement of an entity's structure is severed or substantially transformed - its functions are usually adversely affected. Direct interference with a system's functionality is equally deleterious.

We can render a system dysfunctional by inhibiting or reversing any stage in the complex processes involved - or by preventing the entity's communication with its environs. Another method of annihilation involves the alteration of the entity's context - its surroundings, its codes and signals, its interactive patterns, its potential partners, friends and foes.

Finding the lethal weaknesses of an organism, an apparatus, or a society is described as a process of trial and error. But the outcome is guaranteed: mortal susceptibility is assumed to be a universal trait. No one and nothing is perfectly immune, utterly invulnerable, or beyond extermination.

Yet, what is poison to one species is nectar to another. Water can be either toxic or indispensable, depending on the animal, the automaton, or the system. Scorching temperatures, sulfur emissions, ammonia or absolute lack of oxygen are, to some organisms, the characteristics of inviting habitats. To others, the very same are deadly.

Can we conceive of an indestructible thing - be it unicellular or multicellular, alive or robotic, composed of independent individuals or acting in perfect, centrally-dictated unison? Can anything be, in principle, eternal?

This question is not as outlandish as it sounds. By fighting disease and trying to postpone death, for instance, we aspire to immortality and imperishability. Some of us believe in God - an entity securely beyond ruin. Intuitively, we consider the Universe - if not time and space - to be everlasting, though constantly metamorphosing.

What is common to these examples of infinite resilience is their unbounded and unparalleled size and might. Lesser objects are born or created. Since there has been a time, prior to their genesis, in which they did not exist - it is easy to imagine a future without them.

Even where the distinction between individual and collective is spurious their end is plausible. True, though we can obliterate numerous "individual" bacteria - others, genetically identical, will always survive our onslaught. Yet, should the entire Earth vanish - so would these organisms. The extinction of all bacteria, though predicated on an unlikely event, is still thinkable.

But what about an entity that is "pure energy", a matrix of fields, a thought, immaterial yet very real, omnipresent and present nowhere? Such a being comes perilously close to the divine. For if it is confined to certain space - however immense - it is perishable together with that space. If it is not - then it is God, as perceived by its believers.

But what constitutes "destruction" or "annihilation"? We are familiar with death - widely considered the most common form of inexistence. But some people believe that death is merely a transformation from one state of being to another. Sometimes all the constituents of a system remain intact but cease to interact. Does this amount to obliteration? And what about a machine that stops interacting with its environment altogether - though its internal processes continue unabated. Is it still "functioning"?

It is near impossible to say when a "live" or "functioning" entity ceases to be so. Death is the form of destruction we are most acquainted with. For a discussion of death and the human condition - read this ***Death, Meaning, and Identity***

Return

I, Robot: The Fourth Law of Robotics

The movie "I, Robot" is a muddled affair. It relies on shoddy pseudo-science and a general sense of unease that artificial (non-carbon based) intelligent life forms seem to provoke in us. But it goes no deeper than a comic book treatment of the important themes that it broaches.

Sigmund Freud said that we have an uncanny reaction to the inanimate. This is probably because we know that – pretensions and layers of philosophizing aside – we are nothing but recursive, self aware, introspective, conscious machines. Special machines, no doubt, but machines all the same.

Consider the James bond movies. They constitute a decades-spanning gallery of human paranoia. Villains change: communists, neo-Nazis, media moguls. But one kind of villain is a fixture in this psychodrama, in this parade of human phobias: the machine. James Bond always finds himself confronted with hideous, vicious, malicious machines and automata.

It was precisely to counter this wave of unease, even terror, irrational but all-pervasive, that Isaac Asimov, the late Sci-fi writer (and scientist) invented the Three Laws of Robotics:

1. *A robot may not injure a human being or, through inaction, allow a human being to come to harm.*

2. *A robot must obey the orders given it by human beings, except where such orders would conflict with the First Law.*
3. *A robot must protect its own existence as long as such protection does not conflict with the First or Second Laws.*

Many have noticed the lack of consistency and, therefore, the inapplicability of these laws when considered together.

First, they are not derived from any coherent worldview or background. To be properly implemented and to avoid their interpretation in a potentially dangerous manner, the robots in which they are embedded must be equipped with reasonably comprehensive models of the physical universe and of human society.

Without such contexts, these laws soon lead to intractable paradoxes (experienced as a nervous breakdown by one of Asimov's robots). Conflicts are ruinous in automata based on recursive functions (Turing machines), as all robots are. Godel pointed at one such self destructive paradox in the "Principia Mathematica", ostensibly a comprehensive and self consistent logical system. It was enough to discredit the whole magnificent edifice constructed by Russel and Whitehead over a decade.

Some argue against this and say that robots need not be automata in the classical, Church-Turing, sense. That they could act according to heuristic, probabilistic rules of decision making. There are many other types of functions (non-recursive) that can be incorporated in a robot, they remind us.

True, but then, how can one guarantee that the robot's behavior is fully predictable ? How can one be certain that robots will fully and always implement the three laws? Only recursive systems are predictable in principle, though, at times, their complexity makes it impossible.

This article deals with some commonsense, basic problems raised by the Laws. The next article in this series analyses the Laws from a few vantage points: philosophy, artificial intelligence and some systems theories.

An immediate question springs to mind: ***HOW*** will a robot identify a human being? Surely, in a future of perfect androids, constructed of organic materials, no superficial, outer scanning will suffice. Structure and composition will not be sufficient differentiating factors.

There are two ways to settle this very practical issue: one is to endow the robot with the ability to conduct a Converse Turing Test (to separate humans from other life forms) - the other is to somehow "barcode" all the robots by implanting some remotely readable signaling device inside them (such as a RFID - Radio Frequency ID chip). Both present additional difficulties.

The second solution will prevent the robot from positively identifying humans. He will be able identify with any certainty robots and only robots (or humans with such implants). This is ignoring, for discussion's sake, defects in manufacturing or loss of the implanted identification tags. And what if a robot were to get rid of its tag? Will this also be classified as a "defect in manufacturing"?

In any case, robots will be forced to make a binary choice. They will be compelled to classify one type of physical entities as robots – and all the others as "non-robots". Will non-robots include monkeys and parrots? Yes, unless the manufacturers equip the robots with digital or optical or molecular representations of the human figure (masculine and feminine) in varying positions (standing, sitting, lying down). Or unless all humans are somehow tagged from birth.

These are cumbersome and repulsive solutions and not very effective ones. No dictionary of human forms and positions is likely to be complete. There will always be the odd physical posture which the robot would find impossible to match to its library. A human disk thrower or swimmer may easily be classified as "non-human" by a robot - and so might amputated invalids.

What about administering a converse Turing Test?

This is even more seriously flawed. It is possible to design a test, which robots will apply to distinguish artificial life forms from humans. But it will have to be non-intrusive and not involve overt and prolonged communication. The alternative is a protracted teletype session, with the human concealed behind a curtain, after which the robot will issue its verdict: the respondent is a human or a robot. This is unthinkable.

Moreover, the application of such a test will "humanize" the robot in many important respects. Human identify other humans because they are human, too. This is called empathy. A robot will have to be somewhat human to recognize another human being, it takes one to know one, the saying (rightly) goes.

Let us assume that by some miraculous way the problem is overcome and robots unfailingly identify humans. The next question pertains to the notion of "injury" (still in the First Law). Is it limited only to physical injury (the elimination of the physical continuity of human tissues or of the normal functioning of the human body)?

Should "injury" in the First Law encompass the no less serious mental, verbal and social injuries (after all, they are all known to have physical side effects which are, at times, no less severe than direct physical "injuries")? Is an insult an "injury"? What about being grossly impolite, or psychologically abusive? Or offending religious sensitivities, being politically incorrect - are these injuries? The bulk of human (and, therefore, inhuman) actions actually offend one human being or another, have the potential to do so, or seem to be doing so.

Consider surgery, driving a car, or investing money in the stock exchange. These "innocuous" acts may end in a coma, an accident, or ruinous financial losses, respectively. Should a robot refuse to obey human instructions which may result in injury to the instruction-givers?

Consider a mountain climber – should a robot refuse to hand him his equipment lest he falls off a cliff in an unsuccessful bid to reach the peak? Should a robot refuse to obey human commands pertaining to the crossing of busy roads or to driving (dangerous) sports cars?

Which level of risk should trigger robotic refusal and even prophylactic intervention? At which stage of the interactive man-machine collaboration should it be activated? Should a robot refuse to fetch a ladder or a rope to someone who intends to commit suicide by hanging himself (that's an easy one)?

Should he ignore an instruction to push his master off a cliff (definitely), help him climb the cliff (less assuredly so), drive him to the cliff (maybe so), help him get into his car in order to drive him to the cliff... Where do the responsibility and obeisance bucks stop?

Whatever the answer, one thing is clear: such a robot must be equipped with more than a rudimentary sense of judgment, with the ability to appraise and analyse complex situations, to predict the future and to base his decisions on very fuzzy algorithms (no programmer can foresee all possible circumstances). To me, such a "robot" sounds much more dangerous (and humanoid) than any recursive automaton which does **NOT** include the famous Three Laws.

Moreover, what, exactly, constitutes "inaction"? How can we set apart inaction from failed action or, worse, from an action which failed by design, intentionally? If a human is in danger and the robot tries to save him and fails – how could we determine to what extent it exerted itself and did everything it could?

How much of the responsibility for a robot's inaction or partial action or failed action should be imputed to the manufacturer – and how much to the robot itself? When a robot decides finally to ignore its own programming – how are we to gain information regarding this momentous event? Outside appearances can hardly be expected to help us distinguish a rebellious robot from a lackadaisical one.

The situation gets much more complicated when we consider states of conflict.

Imagine that a robot is obliged to harm one human in order to prevent him from hurting another. The Laws are absolutely inadequate in this case. The robot should either establish an empirical hierarchy of injuries – or an empirical hierarchy of humans. Should we, as humans, rely on robots or on their manufacturers (however wise, moral and compassionate) to make this selection for us? Should we abide by their judgment which injury is the more serious and warrants an intervention?

A summary of the Asimov Laws would give us the following "truth table":

A robot must obey human commands except if:

1. Obeying them is likely to cause injury to a human, or
2. Obeying them will let a human be injured.

A robot must protect its own existence with three exceptions:

1. That such self-protection is injurious to a human;
2. That such self-protection entails inaction in the face of potential injury to a human;
3. That such self-protection results in robot insubordination (failing to obey human instructions).

Trying to create a truth table based on these conditions is the best way to demonstrate the problematic nature of Asimov's idealized yet highly impractical world.

Here is an exercise:

Imagine a situation (consider the example below or one you make up) and then create a truth table based on the above five conditions. In such a truth table, "T" would stand for "compliance" and "F" for non-compliance.

Example:

A radioactivity monitoring robot malfunctions. If it self-destructs, its human operator might be injured. If it does not, its malfunction will equally seriously injure a patient dependent on his performance.

One of the possible solutions is, of course, to introduce gradations, a probability calculus, or a utility calculus. As they are phrased by Asimov, the rules and conditions are of a threshold, yes or no, take it or leave it nature. But if robots were to be instructed to maximize overall utility, many borderline cases would be resolved.

Still, even the introduction of heuristics, probability, and utility does not help us resolve the dilemma in the example above. Life is about inventing new rules on the fly, as we go, and as we encounter new challenges in a kaleidoscopically metamorphosing world. Robots with rigid instruction sets are ill suited to cope with that.

Note - Godel's Theorems

The work of an important, though eccentric, Czech-Austrian mathematical logician, Kurt Gödel (1906-1978) dealt with the completeness and consistency of logical systems. A passing acquaintance with his two theorems would have saved the architect a lot of time.

Gödel's First Incompleteness Theorem states that every consistent axiomatic logical system, sufficient to express arithmetic, contains true but unprovable ("not decidable") sentences. In certain cases (when the system is omega-consistent), both said sentences and their negation are unprovable. The system is consistent and true - but not "complete" because not all its sentences can be decided as true or false by either being proved or by being refuted.

The Second Incompleteness Theorem is even more earth-shattering. It says that no consistent formal logical system can prove its own consistency. The system may be complete - but then we are unable to show, using its axioms and inference laws, that it is consistent

In other words, a computational system can either be complete and inconsistent - or consistent and incomplete. By trying to construct a system both complete and consistent, a robotics engineer would run afoul of Gödel's theorem.

Note - Turing Machines

In 1936 an American (Alonzo Church) and a Briton (Alan M. Turing) published independently (as is often the case in science) the basics of a new branch in Mathematics (and logic): computability or recursive functions (later to be developed into Automata Theory).

The authors confined themselves to dealing with computations which involved "effective" or "mechanical" methods for finding results (which could also be expressed as solutions (values) to formulae). These methods were so called because they could, in principle, be performed by simple machines (or human-computers or human-calculators, to use Turing's unfortunate phrases). The emphasis was on finiteness: a finite number of instructions, a finite number of symbols in each instruction, a finite number of steps to the result. This is why these methods were usable by humans without the aid of an apparatus (with the exception of pencil and paper as memory aids). Moreover: no insight or ingenuity were allowed to "interfere" or to be part of the solution seeking process.

What Church and Turing did was to construct a set of all the functions whose values could be obtained by applying effective or mechanical calculation methods. Turing went further down Church's road and designed the "Turing Machine" – a machine which can calculate the values of all the functions whose values can be found using effective or mechanical methods. Thus, the program running the TM (=Turing Machine in the rest of this text) was really an effective or mechanical method. For the initiated readers: Church solved the decision-problem for propositional calculus and Turing proved that there is no solution to the decision problem relating to the predicate calculus. Put more simply, it is possible to "prove" the truth value (or the theorem status) of an expression in the propositional calculus – but not in the predicate calculus. Later it was shown that many functions (even in number theory itself) were not recursive, meaning that they could not be solved by a Turing Machine.

No one succeeded to prove that a function must be recursive in order to be effectively calculable. This is (as Post noted) a "working hypothesis" supported by overwhelming evidence. We don't know of any effectively calculable function which is not recursive, by designing new TMs from existing ones we can obtain new effectively calculable functions from existing ones and TM computability stars in every attempt to understand effective calculability (or these attempts are reducible or equivalent to TM computable functions).

The Turing Machine itself, though abstract, has many "real world" features. It is a blueprint for a computing device with one "ideal" exception: its unbounded memory (the tape is infinite). Despite its hardware appearance (a read/write head which scans a two-dimensional tape inscribed with ones and zeroes, etc.) – it is really a software application, in today's terminology. It carries out instructions, reads and writes, counts and so on. It is an automaton designed to implement an effective or mechanical method of solving functions (determining the truth value of propositions). If the transition from input to output is deterministic we have a classical automaton – if it is determined by a table of probabilities – we have a probabilistic automaton.

With time and hype, the limitations of TMs were forgotten. No one can say that the Mind is a TM because no one can prove that it is engaged in solving only recursive functions. We can say that TMs can do whatever digital computers are doing – but not that digital computers are TMs by definition. Maybe they are – maybe they are not. We do not know enough about them and about their future.

Moreover, the demand that recursive functions be computable by an UNAIDED human seems to restrict possible equivalents. Inasmuch as computers emulate human computation (Turing did believe so when he helped construct the ACE, at the time the fastest computer in the world) – they are TMs. Functions whose values are calculated by AIDED humans with the contribution of a computer are still recursive. It is when humans are aided by other kinds of instruments that we have a problem. If we use measuring devices to determine the values of a function it does not seem to conform to the definition of a recursive function. So, we can generalize and say that functions whose values are calculated by an AIDED human could be recursive, depending on the apparatus used and on the lack of ingenuity or insight (the latter being, anyhow, a weak, non-rigorous requirement which cannot be formalized).

Also Read

Intuition

On Empathy

On Being Human

The Interrupted Self

Narcissist, the Machine

Being John Malkovich

The Shattered Identity

The Chinese Room Revisited

Turing Machines and Universes

The Metaphors of the Mind - Part I (The Brain)

Return

The Interrupted Self

In the futuristic sci-fi film "Surrogates" (2009), people stay at home, their nervous system wired to allow them to remote control a robot, their surrogate. The robot and its operator, the human being, are an ontological unity: both share identical, objective experiences. There is one exception: when something bad happens to the robot, its owner is shielded from the consequences by some kind of "firewall", or in-built defense.

Inevitably, things go awry. The design of the robots is unwise: they retain the long-term memories of their masters, which renders them susceptible to malicious hacking; they possess superhuman faculties, which makes them resistant to law enforcement efforts; and in appearance, they are not clones of their owners, which results in mayhem.

The film also ignores the discontinuities of human life: the natural functions of eating, washing, and excretion, or the onset of boredom and attention deficits. It is not clear what the robots are supposed to do when nature calls and how their operators resume the session where it had stopped and pick up their ruptured train of thought.

The movie raises numerous fascinating questions, not the least of which is:

When the owner of a surrogate, cocooned in his den, uses his contraption to visit China, or to have sex, or to stroll along a boulevard - who does the experiencing? Can one really say that one has been to China, or has had sex, or has strolled along a boulevard in autumn if one has never left the comfort of one's home? If one's body is stationary and only one's mind is wandering and acting through a technological extension, does this constitute "being there" and "doing it"?

In the film, it is not made clear whether the brains of the operators of the surrogates are induced to react as they would in "real"-life situations: as the surrogates go about their business, do their owners sweat, smell, and feel pressure, for instance? Do they experience non-life-threatening short breath and elevated heart rate? Do they truly ejaculate? Yet, having gone this far, it is easy to imagine a device that would stimulate the right brain centers to produce these reactions.

Once the experiences of having sex or touring China via such a machine become indistinguishable from the real thing, in which sense are they "less real"? Isn't it all in the mind, in any case? This is the famous "brain in a jar" conundrum: if one's brain were to be placed in a jar and sustained artificially, would one still be capable of experiencing life fully and in which sense would one exist in such "reduced" circumstances? Wouldn't then the brain-support apparatus constitute the full equivalent of one's erstwhile body, only far less fallible and prone to dysfunction?

The hidden and misleading assumption in all these thought experiments is that the brain and its flesh-and-blood container were once united, before science or technology had them sundered. But what about a human brain that has never had a body? A brain that was grown in a jar or rigged to a surrogate from its very inception? Would such a "monstrosity" qualify as an individual member of the human species? In other words: how important is the body to the formation and operation of the mind?

The dualistic differentiation between mens and corpus may be entirely artificial. It seems to be the outcome of our ignorance and of the shortcomings of our language, both of which gave rise to the psychophysical problem.

In a series of experiments described in articles published in Science in mid 2007, British and Swiss researchers concluded that *"their experiments reinforce the idea that the 'self' is closely tied to a 'within-body' position, which is dependent on information from the senses. 'We look at 'self' with regard to spatial characteristics, and maybe they form the basis upon which self-consciousness has evolved'"*, one of them told the New Scientist ("Out-of-body experiences are 'all in the mind'", NewScientist.com news service, 23 August 2007).

The fundament of our mind and of our self is the mental map we create of our body ("Body Image", or "Body Map"). It is a detailed, psychic, rendition of our corporeal self, based on sensa (sensory input) and above all on proprioception and other kinesthetic senses. This model incorporates representations of other objects and results, at a higher level, in a "World Map" or "World Image". This World Map often does not react to actual changes in the body itself (such as amputation which results in the "phantom limb" phenomenon). It is also exclusionary of facts that contradict the paradigm at the basis of the World Map.

This detailed and ever-changing (dynamic) map constitutes the set of outer constraints and threshold conditions for the brain's operations. The triple processes of interaction (endogenous and exogenous), integration (assimilation) and accommodation (see here "Psychophysics") reconcile the brain's "programmes" (sets of instructions) to these constraints and conditions.

In other words, these are processes of solving dynamic, though always partial, equations. The set of all the solutions to all these equations constitutes the "Personal Narrative", or "Personality". Thus, "organic" and "mental" disorders (a dubious distinction at best) have many characteristics in common (confabulation, antisocial behaviour, emotional absence or flatness, indifference, psychotic episodes and so on).

The brain's "Functional Set" is hierarchical and consists of feedback loops. It aspires to equilibrium and homeostasis. The most basic level is mechanical: hardware (neurons, glia, etc.) and operating system software. This software consists of a group of sensory-motor applications. It is separated from the next level by exegetic instructions (the feedback loops and their interpretation). This is the cerebral equivalent of a compiler. Each level of instructions is distinguished from the next (and connected to it meaningfully and operationally) by such a compiler. Here, again, the "body" *is* the mind!

Next follow the "functional instructions" ("How to" type of commands): how to see, how to place visuals in context, how to hear, how to collate and correlate sensory input and so on. Yet, these commands should not be confused with the "real thing", the "final product". "How-to-see" is not the same as "seeing". Seeing is a much more complex, multilayered, interactive and versatile "activity" than the simple act of light penetration and its conveyance to the brain.

Thus - separated by another compiler which generates meanings (a "dictionary") - we reach the realm of "meta-instructions". This is a gigantic classificatory (taxonomic) system. It contains and applies rules of symmetry (left vs. right), physics (light vs. dark, colors), social codes (face recognition, behaviour) and synergetic or correlated activity ("seeing", "music", etc.).

Design principles would yield the application of the following principles to the organization and architecture of the brain:

1. Areas of specialization (dedicated to hearing, reading, smelling, etc.);

2. Redundancy (unutilized over capacity capable to taking over functions from damaged centers);

3. Holography and Fractalness (replication of same mechanisms, sets of instructions and some critical content in various locations in the brain);

4. Interchangeability - Higher functions can replace damaged lower ones (seeing can replace damaged proprioception, for instance).

5. Two types of processes:

a. Rational - discrete, atomistic, syllogistic, theory-constructing, falsifying;
b. Emotional - continuous, fractal, holographic.

By "fractal and holographic", I mean:

1. That each part contains the total information about the whole;

2. That each unit or part contain a "connector" to all others with sufficient information in such a connector to reconstruct the other units if lost or unavailable.

Only some brain processes are "conscious". Others, though equally complex (e.g., semantic interpretation of spoken texts), may be unconscious. The same brain processes can be conscious at one time and unconscious at another. Consciousness, in other words, is the privileged tip of a submerged mental iceberg.

One hypothesis is that an uncounted number of unconscious processes "yield" conscious processes. This is the emergent phenomenal (epiphenomenal) "wave-particle" duality. Unconscious brain processes are like a wave function which collapses into the "particle" of consciousness.

Another hypothesis, more closely aligned with tests and experiments, is that consciousness is like a searchlight. It focuses on a few "privileged processes" at a time and thus makes them conscious. As the light of consciousness moves on, new privileged processes (hitherto unconscious) become conscious and the old ones recede into unconsciousness.

We tend to ignore the fact that the mind is somehow entangled with the brain and that the brain is "hardware", an integral part of the body. It is the body that gives rise to the mind. Without it, the mind would be so different that it could scarcely qualify as human. We are human because we have bodies. In the rarefied atmosphere of academe, this crucial observation is often neglected or wilfully ignored.

Also Read:

Psychophysics

Return

The Ecology of Environmentalism

"It wasn't just predictable curmudgeons like Dr. Johnson who thought the Scottish hills ugly; if anybody had something to say about mountains at all, it was sure to be an insult. (The Alps: "monstrous excrescences of nature," in the words of one wholly typical 18th-century observer.)"

Stephen Budiansky, "Nature? A bit overdone", U.S. News & World Report, December 2, 1996

The concept of "nature" is a romantic invention. It was spun by the likes of Jean-Jacques Rousseau in the 18th century as a confabulated utopian contrast to the dystopia of urbanization and Darwinian, ruthless materialism. The traces of this dewy-eyed conception of the "savage", his alleged harmony and resonance with nature, and his unmolested, unadulterated surroundings can be found in the more malignant forms of fundamentalist environmentalism and in pop-culture (the most recent example of which is the propaganda-laden cinematic extravaganza, "Avatar").

At the other extreme are religious literalists who regard Man as the crown of creation with complete dominion over nature and the right to exploit its resources unreservedly. Similar, veiled, sentiments can be found among scientists. The Anthropic Principle, for instance, promoted by many outstanding physicists, claims that the nature of the Universe is preordained to accommodate sentient beings - namely, us humans.

Industrialists, politicians and economists have only recently begun paying lip service to sustainable development and to the environmental costs of their policies. Thus, in a way, they bridge the abyss - at least verbally - between these two diametrically opposed forms of fundamentalism. Similarly, the denizens of the West continue to indulge in rampant consumption, but now it is suffused with environmental guilt rather than driven by unadulterated hedonism.

Still, essential dissimilarities between the schools notwithstanding, the dualism of Man vs. Nature is universally acknowledged.

Modern physics - notably the Copenhagen interpretation of quantum mechanics - has abandoned the classic split between (typically human) observer and (usually inanimate) observed. Environmentalists, in contrast, have embraced this discarded worldview wholeheartedly. To them, Man is the active agent operating upon a distinct reactive or passive substrate - i.e., Nature. But, though intuitively compelling, it is a false dichotomy.

Man is, by definition, a part of Nature. His tools are natural. He interacts with the other elements of Nature and modifies it - but so do all other species. Arguably, bacteria and insects exert on Nature far more influence with farther reaching consequences than Man has ever done.

Still, the "Law of the Minimum" - that there is a limit to human population growth and that this barrier is related to the biotic and abiotic variables of the environment - is undisputed. Whatever debate there is veers between two strands of this Malthusian Weltanschauung: the utilitarian (a.k.a. anthropocentric, shallow, or technocentric) and the ethical (alternatively termed biocentric, deep, or ecocentric).

First, the Utilitarians.

Economists, for instance, tend to discuss the costs and benefits of environmental policies. Activists, on the other hand, demand that Mankind consider the "rights" of other beings and of nature as a whole in determining a least harmful course of action.

Utilitarians regard nature as a set of exhaustible and scarce resources and deal with their optimal allocation from a human point of view. Yet, they usually fail to incorporate intangibles such as the beauty of a sunset or the liberating sensation of open spaces.

"Green" accounting - adjusting the national accounts to reflect environmental data - is still in its unpromising infancy. It is complicated by the fact that ecosystems do not respect man-made borders and by the stubborn refusal of many ecological variables to succumb to numbers. To complicate things further, different nations weigh environmental problems disparately.

Despite recent attempts, such as the Environmental Sustainability Index (ESI) produced by the World Economic Forum (WEF), no one knows how to define and quantify elusive concepts such as "sustainable development". Even the costs of replacing or repairing depleted resources and natural assets are difficult to determine.

Efforts to capture "quality of life" considerations in the straitjacket of the formalism of distributive justice -

known as human-welfare ecology or emancipatory environmentalism - backfired. These led to derisory attempts to reverse the inexorable processes of urbanization and industrialization by introducing localized, small-scale production.

Social ecologists proffer the same prescriptions but with an anarchistic twist. The hierarchical view of nature - with Man at the pinnacle - is a reflection of social relations, they suggest. Dismantle the latter - and you get rid of the former.

The Ethicists appear to be as confounded and ludicrous as their "feet on the ground" opponents.

Biocentrists view nature as possessed of an intrinsic value, regardless of its actual or potential utility. They fail to specify, however, how this, even if true, gives rise to rights and commensurate obligations. Nor was their case aided by their association with the apocalyptic or survivalist school of environmentalism which has developed proto-fascist tendencies and is gradually being scientifically debunked.

The proponents of deep ecology radicalize the ideas of social ecology ad absurdum and postulate a transcendentalist spiritual connection with the inanimate (whatever that may be). In consequence, they refuse to intervene to counter or contain natural processes, including diseases and famine.

The politicization of environmental concerns runs the gamut from political activism to eco-terrorism. The environmental movement - whether in academe, in the media, in non-governmental organizations, or in legislature - is now comprised of a web of bureaucratic interest groups.

Like all bureaucracies, environmental organizations are out to perpetuate themselves, fight heresy and accumulate political clout and the money and perks that come with it. They are no longer a disinterested and objective party. They have a stake in apocalypse. That makes them automatically suspect.

Bjorn Lomborg, author of "The Skeptical Environmentalist", was at the receiving end of such self-serving sanctimony. A statistician, he demonstrated that the doom and gloom tendered by environmental campaigners, scholars and militants are, at best, dubious and, at worst, the outcomes of deliberate manipulation.

The situation is actually improving on many fronts, showed Lomborg: known reserves of fossil fuels and most metals are rising, agricultural production per head is surging, the number of the famished is declining, biodiversity loss is slowing as do pollution and tropical deforestation. In the long run, even in pockets of environmental degradation, in the poor and developing countries, rising incomes and the attendant drop in birth rates will likely ameliorate the situation in the long run.

Yet, both camps, the optimists and the pessimists, rely on partial, irrelevant, or, worse, manipulated data. The multiple authors of "People and Ecosystems", published by the World Resources Institute, the World Bank and the United Nations conclude: "Our knowledge of ecosystems has increased dramatically, but it simply has not kept pace with our ability to alter them."

Quoted by The Economist, Daniel Esty of Yale, the leader of an environmental project sponsored by World Economic Forum, exclaimed:

"Why hasn't anyone done careful environmental measurement before? Businessmen always say, 'what matters gets measured'. Social scientists started quantitative measurement 30 years ago, and even political science turned to hard numbers 15 years ago. Yet look at environmental policy, and the data are lousy."

Nor is this dearth of reliable and unequivocal information likely to end soon. Even the Millennium Ecosystem Assessment, supported by numerous development agencies and environmental groups, is seriously under-financed. The conspiracy-minded attribute this curious void to the self-serving designs of the apocalyptic school of environmentalism. Ignorance and fear, they point out, are among the fanatic's most useful allies. They also make for good copy.

A Comment on Energy Security

The pursuit of "energy security" has brought us to the brink. It is directly responsible for numerous wars, big and small; for unprecedented environmental degradation; for global financial imbalances and meltdowns; for growing income disparities; and for ubiquitous unsustainable development.

It is energy *insecurity* that we should seek.

The uncertainty incumbent in phenomena such "peak oil", or in the preponderance of hydrocarbon fuels in failed states fosters innovation. The more insecure we get, the more we invest in the recycling of energy-rich products; the more substitutes we find for energy-intensive foods; the more we conserve energy; the more we switch to alternatives energy; the more we encourage international collaboration; and the more we optimize energy outputs per unit of fuel input.

A world in which energy (of whatever source) will be abundant and predictably available would suffer from entropy, both physical and mental. The vast majority of human efforts revolve around the need to deploy our meager resources wisely. Energy also serves as a geopolitical "organizing principle" and disciplinary rod. Countries which waste energy (and the money it takes to buy it), pollute, and conflict with energy suppliers end up facing diverse crises, both domestic and foreign. Profligacy is punished precisely because energy in insecure. Energy scarcity and precariousness thus serves a global regulatory mechanism.

But the obsession with "energy security" is only one example of the almost religious belief in "scarcity".

A Comment on Alternative Energies

The quest for alternative, non-fossil fuel, energy sources is driven by two misconceptions: (1) The mistaken belief in "peak oil" (that we are nearing the complete depletion and exhaustion of economically extractable oil reserves) and (2) That market mechanisms cannot be trusted to provide adequate and timely responses to energy needs (in other words that markets are prone to failure).

At the end of the 19th century, books and pamphlets were written about "peak coal". People and governments panicked: what would satisfy the swelling demand for energy? Apocalyptic thinking was rampant. Then, of course, came oil. At first, no one knew what to do with the sticky, noxious, and occasionally flammable substance. Gradually, petroleum became our energetic mainstay and gave rise to entire industries (petrochemicals and automotive, to mention but two).

History will repeat itself: the next major source of energy is very unlikely to be hatched up in a laboratory. It will be found fortuitously and serendipitously. It will shock and surprise pundits and laymen alike. And it will amply cater to all our foreseeable needs. It is also likely to be greener than carbon-based fuels.

More generally, the market can take care of itself: energy does not have the characteristics of a public good and therefore is rarely subject to market breakdowns and unalleviated scarcity. Energy prices have proven themselves to be a sagacious regulator and a perspicacious invisible hand.

Until this holy grail ("the next major source of energy") reveals itself, we are likely to increase the shares of nuclear and wind sources in our energy consumption pie. Our industries and cars will grow even more energy-efficient. But there is no escaping the fact that the main drivers of global warming and climate change are population growth and the emergence of an energy-guzzling middle class in developing and formerly poor countries. These are irreversible economic processes and only at their inception.

Global warming will, therefore, continue apace no matter which sources of energy we deploy. It is inevitable. Rather than trying to limit it in vain, we would do better to adapt ourselves: avoid the risks and cope with them while also reaping the rewards (and, yes, climate change has many positive and beneficial aspects to it).

Climate change is not about the demise of the human species as numerous self-interested (and well-paid) alarmists would have it. Climate change is about the global redistribution and reallocation of economic resources. No wonder the losers are sore and hysterical. It is time to consider the winners, too and hear their hitherto muted voices. Alternative energy is nice and all but it is rather besides the point and it misses both the big picture and the trends that will make a difference in this century and the next.

Note on Adapting to Climate Change

How must society adapt to rapid climate change to minimize severe upheaval?

The question makes two explicit assumptions, both of which are controversial and disputed: that climate change is rapid and that it will result in severe upheaval. Similarly, it is not clear whether the best reaction to global warming should be societal, or individual (or, perhaps, global).

That global warming is happening has now been established. Yet, such a forcing is likely to take centuries to induce any discernible climate change on the planetary level. Moreover: self-interested and well-paying hype aside, we know close to nothing about the hypercomplex set of interactions between various greenhouse gases, the atmosphere, the oceans, the Earth's orbit, volcanic eruptions, human activities, the unforeseen outcomes and by-products of well-meaning regulation and technologies (such as biofuels), solar dynamics, plate tectonics, and thousands of other factors, the vast majority of which are yet to be discovered.

Environmentalism is, therefore, poor science or pseudo-science: it is a pernicious and venal form of faddish hubris. In our current state of ignorance, the more ambitious variants of "solutions" such as geoengineering are far more dangerous than the threats of global warming.

Two things are clear, though: (a) Climate change had happened frequently and repeatedly, long before and ever since humans strode the scene; and (b) Some regions of

Earth will greatly benefit economically from global warming. Others, inevitably, will suffer and will have to adapt. None of this sounds like a "severe upheaval", let alone life-threatening as the more rabid and sensationalist environmentalists will have us believe.

We should take an inventory of what we know and act upon it resolutely (mitigation): emissions from fossil fuel combustion should be tamed, captured, stored, sunk, and sequestered (aerosols to be further studied in conjunction with global dimming and ozone depletion); measures for population control and family planning enhanced; alternative and renewable fuels should be studied and incentives provided to energy-efficient, clean and green technologies; cement manufacture should be tweaked; cap and trade (or tax) schemes implemented on the national, corporate, and individual levels; weather-resistant, energy-conserving, and green construction technologies pioneered; the diets of livestock should be adapted to restrict biological emissions; deforestation and reforestation should be rationalized as should be land use; drought-related indigenous agricultural and water management knowledge and crop varieties should be preserved; flood defenses erected or strengthened; and weather-monitoring capacity should be extended and modernized. These measures make good sense, whatever the urgency of the problem facing us.

But, we should invest the bulk of our scarce resources in research and innovation. We should accept that climate change is inevitable and work out ways of harnessing it to our benefit. We should come up with new agricultural methods and strains; new types of tourism; new irrigation techniques; water desalination, diversion, transport, and allocation schemes; ways of sustaining biological diversity and of helping the human body adapt and cope; and global plans to cope with energy production problems, poverty, and disease triggered by global warming.

For the next few centuries, global warming is inexorable and largely irreversible (as the IPCC essentially admits). To think otherwise is completely delusional. Better to re-imagine our existence on this planet (adaptation). As temperatures rise in certain locales (and drop in others!), new economic activities and routes of commerce would be made possible or rendered feasible; new types of produce and forests will flourish; new technologies will be developed to cater to a novel and growing set of needs.

We would do well to not consider global warming as a crisis, but as a massive change. And even if we insist on regarding it as a cataclysm, as the Chinese saying goes, there are opportunities in every predicament. The initial costs of every transformation and transition in human history have been steep (recall the Industrial Revolution and, more recently, the transition from Communism to Capitalism). Climate change is not likely to be the only exception. Such a massive realignment implies severe disruption and great distress. But, invariably, tectonic shifts are followed by an extended period of creativity and growth. This time will be no different.

Also Read:

The Misconception of Scarcity

The Self-Appointed Altruists

Burning the Oil - Development and Ethnic Tensions

The Emerging Water Wars

Negentropic Agents and the Increase of Entropy

Return

Fact and Truth

The extent of confusion that reigns when we discuss the concept of truth is evident in the film "The Invention of Lying". The movie takes place in a world where people are genetically unable to lie. When one of them, presumably an aberrant mutant (his son inherits his newfound ability), stumbles across the art of confabulation, his life is transformed overnight: he becomes rich, a celebrity, and marries the girl of his dreams (who scorned him before).

But, this clever piece of comedy is philosophically muddled. The denizens of this dystopian cosmos (yes, the truth hurts) not only respond veraciously when prompted – they actually and often sadistically share their innermost thoughts, opinions, and observations. The film fails to realize that volunteering the truth is not the same as being truthful.

What's worse, the characters in the movie take all statements about the future to be true. Yet, statements about the future can be and often are false even in a world where lying is unknown. As Aristotle has put it: nothing we say about the future has a truth value (can be confidently and rigorously determined to be true or false). We can lie only by making statements that we know with certainty to be false, but such certainty exists only with regard to the past and the present. We can make statements about the future that may be false, or that are probably false, or that we believe to be false – but we can never be sure that they are false. Therefore, we can never lie (or tell the truth!) about the future.

Still, it is not as simple as that. Truth must also be possible (there is no such thing as an impossible truth, though, of course, there are many improbable truths). Yet, the very concept of possibility has to do with the future. Moreover: only facts are possible. If something is not possible it is also not factual and nothing that is a fact is impossible.

Consider the following:

Thought experiments (Gedankenexperimenten) are "facts" in the sense that they have a "real life" correlate in the form of electrochemical activity in the brain. But it is quite obvious that they do not relate to facts "out there". They are not true statements.

But do they lack truth because they do not relate to facts? How are Truth and Fact interrelated?

One answer is that Truth pertains to the possibility that an event will occur. If true – it must occur and if false – it cannot occur. This is a binary world of extreme existential conditions. Must all possible events occur? Of course not. If they do not occur would they still be true? Must a statement have a real life correlate to be true?

Instinctively, the answer is yes. We cannot conceive of a thought divorced from brainwaves. A statement which remains a mere potential seems to exist only in the nether land between truth and falsity. It becomes true only by materializing, by occurring, by matching up with real life. If we could prove that it will never do so, we would have felt justified in classifying it as false. This is the outgrowth of millennia of concrete, Aristotelian logic. Logical statements talk about the world and, therefore, if a statement cannot be shown to relate directly to the world, it is not true.

This approach, however, is the outcome of some underlying assumptions:

First, that the world is finite and also close to its end. To say that something that did not happen cannot be true is to say that it will never happen (i.e., to say that time and space – the world – are finite and are about to end momentarily).

Second, truth and falsity are assumed to be mutually exclusive. Quantum and fuzzy logics have long laid this one to rest. There are real world situations that are both true and not-true. A particle can "be" in two places at the same time. This fuzzy logic is incompatible with our daily experiences but if there is anything that we have learnt from physics in the last seven decades it is that the world is incompatible with our daily experiences.

The third assumption is that the psychic realm is but a subset of the material one. We are membranes with a very particular hole-size. We filter through only well defined types of experiences, are equipped with limited (and evolutionarily biased) senses, programmed in a way which tends to sustain us until we die. We are not neutral, objective observers. Actually, the very concept of observer is disputable – as modern physics, on the one hand and Eastern philosophy, on the other hand, have shown.

Imagine that a mad scientist has succeeded to infuse all the water in the world with a strong hallucinogen. At a given moment, all the people in the world see a huge flying saucer. What can we say about this saucer? Is it true? Is it "real"?

There is little doubt that the saucer does not exist. But who is to say so? If this statement is left unsaid – does it mean that it cannot exist and, therefore, is untrue? In this case (of the illusionary flying saucer), the statement that remains unsaid is a true statement – and the statement that is uttered by millions is patently false.

Still, the argument can be made that the flying saucer did exist – though only in the minds of those who drank the contaminated water. What is this form of existence? In which sense does a hallucination "exist"? The psychophysical problem is that no causal relationship can be established between a thought and its real life correlate, the brainwaves that accompany it. Moreover, this leads to infinite regression. If the brainwaves created the thought – who created them, who made them happen? In other words: who is it (perhaps what is it) that thinks?

The subject is so convoluted that to say that the mental is a mere subset of the material is to speculate

It is, therefore, advisable to separate the ontological from the epistemological. But which is which? Facts are determined epistemologically and statistically by conscious and intelligent observers. Their "existence" rests on a sound epistemological footing. Yet we assume that in the absence of observers facts will continue their existence, will not lose their "factuality", their real life quality which is observer-independent and invariant.

What about truth? Surely, it rests on solid ontological foundations. Something is or is not true in reality and that is it. But then we saw that truth is determined psychically and, therefore, is vulnerable, for instance, to hallucinations. Moreover, the blurring of the lines in Quantum, non-Aristotelian, logics implies one of two: either that true and false are only "in our heads" (epistemological) – or that something is wrong with our interpretation of the world, with our exegetic mechanism (brain). If the latter case is true that the world does contain mutually exclusive true and false values – but the organ which identifies these entities (the brain) has gone awry. The paradox is that the second approach also assumes that at least the perception of true and false values is dependent on the existence of an epistemological detection device.

Can something be true and reality and false in our minds? Of course it can (remember "Rashomon"). Could the reverse be true? Yes, it can. This is what we call optical or sensory illusions. Even solidity is an illusion of our senses – there are no such things as solid objects (remember the physicist's desk which is 99.99999% vacuum with minute granules of matter floating about).

To reconcile these two concepts, we must let go of the old belief (probably vital to our sanity) that we can know the world. We probably cannot and this is the source of our confusion. The world may be inhabited by "true" things and "false" things. It may be true that truth is existence and falsity is non-existence. But we will never know because we are incapable of knowing anything about the world as it is.

We are, however, fully equipped to know about the mental events inside our heads. It is there that the representations of the real world form. We are acquainted with these representations (concepts, images, symbols, language in general) – and mistake them for the world itself. Since we have no way of directly knowing the world (without the intervention of our interpretative mechanisms) we are unable to tell when a certain representation corresponds to an event which is observer-independent and invariant and when it corresponds to nothing of the kind. When we see an image – it could be the result of an interaction with light outside us (objectively "real"), or the result of a dream, a drug induced illusion, fatigue and any other number of brain events not correlated with the real world. These are observer-dependent phenomena and, subject to an agreement between a sufficient number of observers, they are judged to be true or "to have happened" (e.g., religious miracles).

To ask if something is true or not is not a meaningful question unless it relates to our internal world and to our capacity as observers. When we say "true" we mean "exists", or "existed", or "most definitely will exist" (the sun will rise tomorrow). But existence can only be ascertained in our minds. Truth, therefore, is nothing but a state of mind. Existence is determined by observing and comparing the two (the outside and the inside, the real and the mental). This yields a picture of the world which may be closely correlated to reality – and, yet again, may not.

Return

The American Hostel

The movie "Hostel" (2005) is a potent depiction of gore and graphic horror. More subtly, it is also a counterfactual and jingoistic political allegory for the post 9-11 age.

A couple of wholesome American youths (one of them a Jew) are nabbed by a ring of east Europeans who cater to the depraved needs of sadists by providing them with fresh supplies of torture victims. The good guys are invariably American (or mistaken for Americans, or the allies of Americans, Japanese). The bad guys are invariably European; a decadent and unfaithful Icelandic, seductive Czech and Russian women, a Dr. Mengele type German, a Ukrainian pimp. The torture chambers are located in a small village in the outskirts of Bratislava, the capital of Slovakia in Central Europe. Everyone is in on the take, the police especially.

The events depicted in the film are not without historical precedent, but the moviemakers got the locations all wrong: nine of ten serial killers worldwide are born and bred in the United States. Born Killers is an American phenomenon, not a European one.

Moreover, the New Europe (to borrow the American Secretary of Defense's unforgettable coinage) - namely, the countries of eastern and central Europe - are obsequious vassals of the United States. It is the Old Europe that regards the United States and its inhabitants as a menace to world peace and stability and a clear and present danger to us all.

Indeed, the United States, as Nobel prize winner Harold Pinter recently pointed out in his acceptance speech, is an evil and psychopathic polity. Niall Ferguson, the renowned historian, claims that from its very inception, the USA set out to cannibalize its neighbors and prey on the weak while amassing wealth and territories in the process.

Like any psychopath, the USA believes that it should be immune to the consequences of its misconduct abroad. Hence its shock when al-Qaida brought the blazing message home: you are not beyond reach. Hence America's insistence that its military and intelligence services - frequently busy raping (Japan, the Philippines), murdering (Vietnam, Kosovo, Iraq, Afghanistan), and pillaging (Iraq) - be exempted from international law and the remit of the International Criminal Court.

The (American) protagonist in the movie gets sliced up but, against all odds, succeeds to extract the badly mutilated Japanese from her hellish cell and escape. Catching a glimpse of her eyeless self, she later commits suicide. Indomitable, he then proceed to torture and amputate the sinister ringleader, a Central European-vaguely German, respectable-looking, middle-class type. He is too late so save his Jewish friend, though (a not so veiled reference to the Holocaust).

This is how Americans view themselves: as good-hearted, good-natured, naive, somewhat gullible, fun-loving, and generous people universally victimized by inscrutable and malevolent foreigners, bent on sadistic and needless destruction. Denial is a defense mechanism very common among narcissists and psychopaths. The truth is, of course, radically different.

With the exception of World War II, the United States has acted as a rapacious conqueror of other peoples' lands under the flimsiest of pretexts. Its expansion was always violent and involved numerous acts of genocide and warfare. Now it is gradually eroding its only redeeming feature: its democracy. It is slowly being transformed from republic to empire, as did Rome two thousand years ago.

The USA is a terrorist state. While there is no disputing that the abhorrent al-Qaida network of murderers should be hunted down and exterminated mercilessly - it is equally morally commendable to wish for the dissolution of the United States and for its disintegration into its constituent states. Pax without Americana is the best of all worlds.

Also Read

[The Roots of Anti-Americanism](#)

[The Semi-failed State](#)

[The Second Civil War](#)

[The Reluctant Empire](#)

[To Give with Grace](#)

[In God We Trust](#)

[The Sergeant and the Girl](#)

[Containing the United States](#)

[Democracy and New Colonialism](#)

Add Me to the List, Mr. Blair

Narcissism, Group Behavior, and Terrorism

The Iraqi and the Madman

Islam and Liberalism

Return

Inception and Its Errors

In the film "Inception", Dom Cobb, is an "extractor": he steals confidential information by hacking into a subject's brain during a dream and conning the victim into disclosing his secrets. This intellectually-challenging and visually-captivating film makes a series of assumptions, none of which withstands close scrutiny:

1. Dream-sharing

The film's fundamental assumption is that dreams are objective entities, akin to buildings whose existence is independent of the observer and are, therefore, accessible to all and sundry. But dreams are highly subjective experiences. External and internal cues are interpreted by and integrated into complex, shape-shifting and highly-idiosyncratic neural networks resident in the head of the dreaming individual. One cannot "tap" into another person's subjectivity (thoughts, emotions, dreams), even in principle (this is the infamous problem of Intersubjectivity). While we can communicate and discuss our inner world, we cannot share it in any meaningful sense, we cannot invite visitors or tourists there. Lucid and directed dreaming is possible, but dream-sharing is not. If we were to enter someone else's mind, we would merely experience our reactions to her mind and not the mind itself.

Intersubjectivity is defined thus by *"The Oxford Companion to Philosophy"(1995)*:

"(Intersubjectivity) refers to the status of being somehow accessible to at least two (usually all, in principle) minds or 'subjectivities'. It thus implies that there is some sort of communication between those minds; which in turn implies that each communicating minds aware not only of the existence of the other but also of its intention to convey information to the other. The idea, for theorists, is that if subjective processes can be brought into agreement, then perhaps that is as good as the (unattainable?) status of being objective - completely independent of subjectivity. The question facing such theorists is whether intersubjectivity is definable without presupposing an objective environment in which communication takes place (the 'wiring' from subject A to subject B). At a less fundamental level, however, the need for intersubjective verification of scientific hypotheses has been long recognized". (Page 414).

2. Defenses and Dreams

The film cannot make up its mind: Cobb tells the aptly-named Ariadne, the "architect" (dream-designer) that the dreaming person's defences are down and all vigilance is gone. This vulnerability makes possible the art of extraction and renders counter-extraction (aka neurosecurity, defensive tactics against thieving extractors) a necessity.

Yet, throughout the movie, the invaded subject's "subconscious" (should be "unconscious") keeps attacking the extraction team. It keeps sending out hostile, violent, and murderous "projections" (figments) to eliminate them. Cobb even compares these apparitions to white blood cells! So, which is it in a dream state: defences down or defences at a maximum?

As Freud, the surrealists and Dadaists knew well, dreams are audio-visual manifestations of the unconscious, the seat of all [psychological defense mechanisms](). In dreams, we are hypervigilant and paranoid. One cannot compel a subject to reveal secrets even under hypnosis, let alone while dreaming. Moreover: dreams provide access only to the unconscious – but, secrets reside exclusively in the conscious part of the mind! The extractors are looking for confidential information in the wrong place!

Finally, dreams use symbols and representations and require interpretations. Even the most pedestrian information is thoroughly encrypted using a highly private language. The film errs in that it depicts dreams as merely "augmented reality", albeit of a highly imaginative and creative sort. Dreams are coded messages, not representations of the world. In this sense, every dreaming person is a solipsist and an [extraterrestrial alien]().

3. Waking up and the stability of dreams

In the film, there are only two or three methods of terminating the dream state and waking up. In reality, the repertoire is unlimited: we wake up for hundreds of reasons including metabolic processes, pain, environmental stimuli, anxiety, compulsive thoughts, circadian awareness, habits, and fears. Dreams are highly unstable states. So unstable, in effect, that many scholars believe that this, precisely, is their role: to keep us alert and on our toes even as we sleep. The use of sedatives (as in the film) actually suppresses dreaming, making them highly counterproductive as far as the extractors are concerned.

4. Dream time dilation

This is a long-discarded myth: dream time is roughly equal to real time. One hour in a dream translates to one "real" hour. It is true, though, that the laws of physics are sometimes suspended while dreaming: distances contract or vanish, for instance. This gives the erroneous impression of time dilation.

5. "Totems" and the reality test

The film warns against the blurring of boundaries and distinctions between dream and reality, especially if one leverages one's memories in the framework of lucid dreaming and incorporates them in the design of new phantasmagorias. Dreamers may lose the reality test and remain unable to tell the two states apart. To guard against this ominous psychosis, extractors use "totems": objects whose behaviour is different in a dream to their true and everyday conduct. Cobb carries a spinning top which, in his dreams, never stops spinning (an oddity which informs him of his slumberous state, of course).

While it is true that objects acquire unfamiliar, even outlandish properties and behaviours in our dreams, their deviations and abnormal characteristics vary from one dream-instance to another and are utterly unpredictable. In one dream, the spinning top will spin forever; in another, it will refuse to spin at all; and, in a third, it will turn into a dove. "Totems", therefore, would be useless as a litmus test. Far better to use a classic "reality check": try to go through a solid object, levitate, look at the face of an analogue clock, or flick a light switch on and off.

Moreover, it is not strictly true that all dreams "feel real" to us. Some dreams do and others don't. We often know that we are dreaming even when we are in the throes of an unfolding visual narrative that is inexorable. We sometimes test ourselves in the dream or even will ourselves to wake up. This ability to tell dream from reality is at the heart of our certainty of which is which.

Nor is it universally true that dreams have no discernible or remembered "beginning" and that we just find ourselves inexplicably immersed in them. The professional literature contains numerous descriptions of dreams with neat beginnings. More often, dreams lack an ending. These absent resolutions and closures provoke and elicit in us psychodynamic processes which are conducive to personal transformation and growth, or even to healing.

6. Nested Dreams

False awakening (dream within a dream) is a documented – albeit, rare – phenomenon. The dreamer usually dreams that he is waking up. There are three caveats, though: (1) Most nested dreams occur in familiar surroundings (one's bed, home, or workplace); (2) The nested dreams share subject matter, some continuity, and a narrative, a plot, or story line; and (3) Invariably the dreamer realises that he is dreaming. Only the second condition is met, to a limited extent, in the film.

7. Creation vs. Discovery or Inspiration

Everyone around Cobb insist that inception – implanting an idea in someone's dreaming mind so that he feels that he has come up with it once he wakes up – is an impossibility. Dreaming, Arthur says, involves "pure creation". It is a process that feels like discovery or inspiration rather than the laborious and tedious constructs that we come up with while awake. Cobb tells Ariadne that our brain is far more active and more efficiently deployed when we dream (completely untrue, judging by brain wave activity).

According to these cinematic extractors, implanted ideas would, therefore, feel alien absent the essential experiences of "discovery" and "inspiration". The subject is bound to react with violence and aggression to the dimly perceived invasion and mind- or dream-snatching. It is the extractor team's job to avoid these defences against intrusion by convincing the subject that the foreign idea is his. Saying more would constitute a cruel spoiler.

But can we really make the distinction between "our" ideas and ideas we have been exposed to and absorbed, ideas whose source is external? Is this taxonomy of "endogenous" versus "exogenous" correct? The answer is a resounding "no". We cannot reliably attribute our ideas to their various sources and cannot credibly tell their origins. Nor do we try to. We assimilate memes and make them ours because such plagiarism has survival value. The unhindered dissemination of "strange notions" (to borrow Saito's phrase in the film) has untold beneficial effects, as any Internet addict will attest.

Furthermore: inspiration and intuition are often cloaked as reasoning and ratiocination. We feel that certain discoveries, theories, and works of art are the outcomes of our toil and rational investment even when they are actually the tip of an unconscious iceberg. Dreams are no different: when we are in them we obey this or that logic; construct theories about our environment, events, and actors; and assume ownership of our ideas and actions, regardless of their source. We never bother or stop to ask the absurd and unanswerable question: "Wait a minute, whose idea was this in the first place?" and so the premise on which the entire film is built is dubious.

Return

Aliens 'R Us
The Ten Errors of Science Fiction

In all works of science fiction, there are ten hidden assumptions regarding alien races. None of these assumptions is a necessity. None of them makes immanent or inevitable sense. Yet, when we read a sci-fi novel or watch a sci-fi movie we tend to accept all of them as inescapable. They amount to a frame of reference and to a language without which we seem to be unable to relate to all manner of exobiology. We evidently believe that life on Earth is a representative sample and that we can extrapolate its properties and mechanisms of action wide and far across the Universe. The principles of symmetry, isotropy, and homogeneity apply to the physical cosmos: Hydrogen behaves identically in our local galactic neighbourhood as it does in the furthest reaches of the Cosmos. Why shouldn't life be the same?

Which leads us to the first fallacy:

1. Life in the Universe

Alien beings may not be alive in any sense of this ambiguous and loaded word. They may not eat, drink, excrete, reproduce, grow, die, process information, or move. Even here, on Earth, we have examples of such entities (viruses, for instance). Why assume that extrasolar creatures must be endowed with a biology of some kind?

But isn't life as we know it an unavoidable outcome of the growing complexity of organisms? This is begging the question. Multi-cellular entities on Earth are manifestations of Carbon-based biology. We cannot imagine beings whose complexity does not spring from some material (or energy) lattice. But our inability to imagine something, even in principle, is no proof that it cannot or does not exist.

2. The Concept of Structure

Aliens in science fiction are typically anthropomorphic in body and in psyche. They sport a central trunk out of which protrude extremities and a head that rests on a variant of our neck. They possess and are possessed by emotions. They reason and debate exactly as we do. The rare few who bear no resemblance to Homo sapiens are usually pure energy. But, even these are arranged in a matrix that is in principle visible or otherwise measurable. We cannot conceive of entities that completely lack organisation.

Yet, structure and organization are mere language elements. They are "in our head" so to speak. They do not exist in reality. They are the results of our limitations: our inability to grasp the whole at once. We use time, space, and form to cope with the immense amount of information that constitutes the Universe. Our minds slice the world and shape it into manageable bits that can be classified and catalogued. We then postulate the existence of interactions to account for our sense of inexorable time. Other inhabitants of the Cosmos may be completely shapeless, lack boundaries or size, be devoid of structure, and be totally inert.

But isn't structure a precondition for complexity? The answer is a resounding no (see my article "The

Complexity of Simplicity"). Additionally, why assume that sentient beings must be complex? Complexity is one solution. Simplicity is another. Our evolution "chose" the former. Processes in other corners of the Galaxy may prefer the latter.

Even the concept of "race" or "species" is doubtful. Why would aliens have to belong to such taxonomic categories? Why can't we imagine a group of astrobiological specimen, each one constituting a distinct species, sui generis, "custom-made"? Why presume that they all must share the same genetic heritage? For that matter, why should they have a genetic make-up at all? Is our DNA the most efficient method of propagating data across time? This is an extremely chauvinistic supposition.

3. Communication and Interaction

Slaves to our (false) sensation of time, we deny the possibility of simultaneity and require that information travels a finite distance in any given period. This precondition requires us to communicate and interact in order to affect changes in our environment and in our interlocutors: we are forced to transfer and transport information by a variety of means from one point in spacetime to another.

Certain sci-fi works introduce "telepathy" into their imaginary worlds: the instant evocation of content in one mind by another's brain acting on it. But telepathy still assumes some kind of transport mechanism and the separateness of sender and recipient in space and, sometimes in time. No matter how imaginative and creative our literary and scientific endeavours, we are unable to convincingly describe a truly timeless, eventless ecosystem where things don't happen and information is immediately available everywhere, vitiating the need for communication and interaction.

Yet, [modern Quantum Mechanics](#) provides us with exactly this insight: that time and space are illusions, linguistic conventions that are the outcomes of our idiosyncratic (not to say inferior) mental apparatus. The foundations of our reality at the particle level are such that simultaneity is common (entanglement) and even the concept of location is gravely challenged (the Uncertainty Principles; tunnelling and other quantum phenomena). Superior beings may not have to communicate or interact at all.

4. Location

In sci-fi works, aliens are always somewhere, in a given location. Granted, some of them project their image. Others can be in multiple places at the same moment or be part of a colony-like hive. But all extraterrestrial life forms occupy space and time and can be pinpointed to a reasonable degree using scientific instrumentation or human sense organs.

Yet, location – like space and time themselves – is a mere convention. At the particle level, knowing one's location is a tricky business as it precludes information about other properties of the object being observed. Embryonic quantum machines and quantum computers already make use of this fact: that the building blocks of our world cannot be effectively located in either space or time (a phenomenon known as [entanglement](#)).

ET may not have a "home". His "place" may be everywhere and nowhere at the same "time". We can't wrap our head around these possibilities because our cerebral computer comes equipped (at least according to Kant) with software that limits us to its parameters and procedures. Moreover: location is an essential component of our sense of identity and individuality.

5. Separateness

It is impossible for us to deny our separation – physical, temporal, and psychological - from other people. We are individuals with a specific mindset, needs, fears, emotions, priorities, personal history, wishes, and place in the world. Our language is ill-equipped to cope with a different reality. We cannot conceive of sharing a body – let alone a mind - with someone else. Even when we discuss multi-organism coordinated and directional hyperstructures, such as ant or bee colonies, we still distinguish between the components comprising them in terms of individuals. We (at least in the West) insist that we not illusory manifestations of an underlying and more fundamental whole.

Yet, as Eastern philosophy and modern physics tell us our separateness may indeed by nothing more than an illusion, a convenient organizing principle and an operational unit, akin to the cell in a human body. Aliens may have long discarded such amenity, if they availed themselves of it to start with. Non-terrestrials may have dispensed with the notions of individuals and separateness, "whole" and "parts" and may have supplanted them with the – to us – unimaginable.

6. Transportation

If location and separateness are deceptive, what need there is of transportation? Of what use are spaceships? Even if location and separateness are real, why would advanced species need to travel anywhere? Why not simply project themselves or induce action at a distance? We don't travel to our bank – we use online banking. We remote control our televisions, power stations, cranes, and numerous other machines. We videoconference. Why reduce supposedly superior races to the travails of physical, galaxy-hopping missions? The classical answer is: in order to manipulate the environment and control it one needs to be physically present there. But why presuppose that Aliens are interested in manipulating or controlling their surroundings (nature)? Even more fundamentally: why think that Aliens have a will at all?

7. Will and Intention

In all sci-fi works, extraterrestrials want something, desire it, or wish for it. They form intentions and act directionally to achieve their goals. These literary devices pose two related problems: (a) we cannot be sure that the actions of alien beings signify – let alone prove – the existence of volition; and (b) we cannot be sure that aliens lack will and intent even if they do not act at all. Put concisely: actions teach us nothing about the existence or absence of intelligence, volition, intent, planning, foresight, and utilitarian thinking. We don't know if and cannot prove that animals (such as pets) are possessed of a will even when they are acting wilfully. Imagine how much more difficult it would be with visitors from outer space. Attributing will and directionality to ET is a prime example of teleology (the belief that causes are preceded by their effects) and anthropomorphosis (attributing human qualities, motives, emotions, and conduct to non-humans).

Throughout this discussion, it would seem that a goal necessarily implies the existence of an intention (to realize it). A lack of intent leaves only one plausible course of action: automatism. Any action taken in the absence of a manifest intention to act is, by definition, an automatic action.

The converse is also true: automatism prescribes the existence of a sole possible mode of action, a sole possible Nature. With an automatic action, no choice is available, there are no degrees of freedom, or freedom of action. Automatic actions are, ipso facto, deterministic.

Still, the distinction between volitional and automatic actions is not clear-cut.

Consider, for instance, house pets. They engage in a variety of acts. They are goal oriented (seek food, drink, etc.). Are they possessed of a conscious, directional, volition (intent)? Many philosophers argued against such a supposition. Moreover, sometimes end-results and by-products are mistaken for goals. Is the goal of objects to fall down? Gravity is a function of the structure of space-time. When we roll a ball down a slope (which is really what gravitation is all about, according to the General Theory of Relativity) is its "goal" to come to a rest at the bottom? Evidently not. Natural processes are considered to be witless reactions. No intent can be attributed to them because no intelligence can be ascribed to them. Yet, this is true but only at times.

8. Intelligence

We cannot safely deduce that Aliens are intelligent from merely observing their behaviour. It is a fallacy to insist that technology and collaboration are predicated on intelligence. Even on Earth, with a limited sample of Life, we have examples of directional (goal-oriented) and technology-empowered behaviour by non-sentient entities (computers, for instance). Intelligence as we understand it requires <u>introspection and self-awareness</u> and, probably a concept of "self" (see item 5 above: "Separateness").

Still, Aliens – like us – are part of Nature. Is Nature as a whole intelligent (as we humans understand intelligence)? Was it designed by an intelligent being (the "watchmaker" hypothesis)? If it was, is each and every part of Nature endowed with this "watchmaker" intelligence?

Intelligence is hard to define. Still, the most comprehensive approach would be to describe it as the synergetic sum of a host of mental processes (some conscious, some not). These mental processes are concerned with information: its gathering, its accumulation, classification, inter-relation, association, analysis, synthesis, integration, and all other modes of processing and manipulation.

But is this manipulation of information not what natural processes are all about? And if nature is the sum total of all natural processes, aren't we forced to admit that nature is (intrinsically, inherently, of itself) intelligent? The intuitive reaction to these suggestions is bound to be negative. When we use the term "intelligence", we seem not to be concerned with just any kind of intelligence - but with intelligence that is separate from and external to what has to be explained. If both the intelligence and the item that needs explaining are members of the same set, we tend to disregard the intelligence involved and label it as "natural" and, therefore, irrelevant.

Moreover, not everything that is created by an intelligence (however "relevant", or external) is intelligent in itself. Some automatic products of intelligent beings are inanimate and non-intelligent. On the other hand, as any Artificial Intelligence buff would confirm, automata can become intelligent, having crossed a certain quantitative or qualitative level of complexity. The weaker form of this statement is that, beyond a certain quantitative or qualitative level of complexity, it is impossible to tell the automatic from the intelligent. Is Nature automatic, is it intelligent, or on the seam between automata and intelligence?

Nature contains everything and, therefore, contains multiple intelligences. That which contains intelligence is not necessarily intelligent, unless the intelligences contained are functional determinants of the container. Quantum Mechanics (rather, its Copenhagen interpretation) implies that this, precisely, is the case. Intelligent, conscious, observers determine the very existence of subatomic particles, the constituents of all matter-energy. Human (intelligent) activity determines the shape, contents and functioning of the habitat Earth. If other intelligent races populate the universe, this could be the rule, rather than the exception. Nature may, indeed, be intelligent in the sense that it is determined by the intelligent races it contains.

Indeed, goal-orientated behaviour (or behavior that could be explained as goal-orientated) is Nature's hallmark. The question whether automatic or intelligent mechanisms are at work, really deals with an underlying issue, that of consciousness. Are these mechanisms self-aware, introspective? Is intelligence possible without such self-awareness, without the internalized understanding of what it is doing?

9. Artificial vs. Natural

Sci-fi authors sometimes suggest or state that "their" Aliens are natural beings, not machines or artificial entities. They tout the complexity of these life forms to prove that they have emerged naturally and are intelligent. In the apocalyptic works that depict a takeover of Earth by man-made or extraterrestrial automata, the marauders or invaders are described as artificial and, therefore, simpler than the natural species that they are challenging. In many respects, these devices are not intelligent.

Conflating the natural with the complex and the intelligent is wrong, however.

Indeed, complexity rises spontaneously in nature through processes such as self-organization. Emergent phenomena are common as are emergent traits: both are not reducible to basic components, interactions, or properties. Yet, complexity does not indicate the existence of a designer or a design. Complexity does not imply the existence of intelligence and sentient beings. On the contrary, complexity usually points towards a natural source and a random origin.

It is also true that complexity and artificiality are often incompatible. Artificial designs and objects are found only in unexpected ("unnatural") contexts and environments. Natural objects are totally predictable and expected. Artificial creations are efficient and, therefore, simple and parsimonious. Natural objects and processes are not.

As Seth Shostak notes in his excellent essay, titled ["SETI and Intelligent Design"](), evolution experiments with numerous dead ends before it yields a single adapted biological entity. DNA is far from optimized: it contains inordinate amounts of junk. Our bodies come replete with dysfunctional appendages and redundant organs. Lightning bolts emit energy all over the electromagnetic spectrum. Pulsars and interstellar gas clouds spew radiation over the entire radio spectrum. The energy of the Sun is ubiquitous over the entire optical and thermal range. No intelligent engineer - human or not - would be so wasteful.

10. Leadership

Finally and perhaps the most preposterous aspect of the vast majority of the sci-fi oeuvre is the imposition of human social structures and predilections on our galactic roommates. They all seem to have leaders, for instance. Yet, even on Earth we have numerous examples of life forms with no leadership or hierarchy and in which decision-making is decentralized in a kind of parallel processing (consider bacteria and plants for instance). Why do all extraterrestrial species resemble the Nazi party is beyond me.

The Six Arguments against SETI

The various projects that comprise the 45-years old Search for Extraterrestrial Intelligence (SETI) raise two important issues:

(1) Do Aliens exist and

(2) Can we communicate with them?

If they do and we can, how come we never encountered an extraterrestrial, let alone spoken to or corresponded with one?

There are six basic explanations to this apparent conundrum and they are not mutually exclusive:

(1) That Aliens do not exist - *click HERE to read the response*

(2) That the technology they use is far too advanced to be detected by us and, the flip side of this hypothesis, that the technology we us is insufficiently advanced to be noticed by them - *click HERE to read the response*

(3) That we are looking for extraterrestrials at the wrong places - *click HERE to read the response*

(4) That the Aliens are life forms so different to us that we fail to recognize them as sentient beings or to communicate with them - *click HERE to read the response*

(5) That Aliens are trying to communicate with us but constantly fail due to a variety of hindrances, some

structural and some circumstantial - ***click HERE to read the response***

(6) That they are avoiding us because of our misconduct (example: the alleged destruction of the environment) or because of our traits (for instance, our innate belligerence) or because of ethical considerations - ***click HERE to read the response***

Argument Number 1: Aliens do not exist (the Fermi Principle)

The assumption that life has arisen only on Earth is both counterintuitive and unlikely. Rather, it is highly probable that life is an extensive parameter of the Universe. In other words, that it is as pervasive and ubiquitous as are other generative phenomena, such as star formation.

This does not mean that extraterrestrial life and life on Earth are necessarily similar. Environmental determinism and the panspermia hypothesis are far from proven. There is no guarantee that we are not unique, as per the Rare Earth hypothesis. But the likelihood of finding life in one form or another elsewhere and everywhere in the Universe is high.

The widely-accepted mediocrity principle (Earth is a typical planet) and its reification, the controversial Drake (or Sagan) Equation usually predicts the existence of thousands of Alien civilizations - though only a vanishingly small fraction of these are likely to communicate with us.

But, if this is true, to quote Italian-American physicist Enrico Fermi: "where are they?" Fermi postulated that ubiquitous technologically advanced civilizations should be detectable - yet they are not! (The Fermi Paradox).

This paucity of observational evidence may be owing to the fact that our galaxy is old. In ten billion years of its existence, the majority of Alien races are likely to have simply died out or been extinguished by various cataclysmic events. Or maybe older and presumably wiser races are not as bent as we are on acquiring colonies. Remote exploration may have supplanted material probes and physical visits to wild locales such as Earth.

Aliens exist on our very planet. The minds of newborn babies and of animals are as inaccessible to us as would be the minds of little green men and antenna-wielding adductors. Moreover, as we demonstrated in the previous chapter, even adult human beings from the same cultural background are as aliens to one another. Language is an inadequate and blunt instrument when it comes to communicating our inner worlds.

Argument Number 2: Their technology is too advanced

If Aliens really want to communicate with us, why would they use technologies that are incompatible with our level of technological progress? When we discover primitive tribes in the Amazon, do we communicate with them via e-mail or video conferencing - or do we strive to learn their language and modes of communication and emulate them to the best of our ability?

Of course there is always the possibility that we are as far removed from Alien species as ants are from us. We do not attempt to interface with insects. If the gap between us and Alien races in the galaxy is too wide, they are unlikely to want to communicate with us at all.

Argument Number 3: *We are looking in all the wrong places*

If life is, indeed, a defining feature (an extensive property) of our Universe, it should be anisotropically, symmetrically, and equally distributed throughout the vast expanse of space. In other words, never mind where we turn our scientific instruments, we should be able to detect life or traces of life.

Still, technological and budgetary constraints have served to dramatically narrow the scope of the search for intelligent transmissions. Vast swathes of the sky have been omitted from the research agenda as have been many spectrum frequencies. SETI scientists assume that Alien species are as concerned with efficiency as we are and, therefore, unlikely to use certain wasteful methods and frequencies to communicate with us. This assumption of interstellar scarcity is, of course, dubious.

Argument Number 4: *Aliens are too alien to be recognized*

Carbon-based life forms may be an aberration or the rule, no one knows. The diversionist and convergionist schools of evolution are equally speculative as are the basic assumptions of both astrobiology and xenobiology. The rest of the universe may be populated with silicon, or nitrogen-phosphorus based races or with information-waves or contain numerous, non-interacting "shadow biospheres".

Recent discoveries of extremophile unicellular organisms lend credence to the belief that life can exist almost under any circumstances and in all conditions and that the range of planetary habitability is much larger than thought.

But whatever their chemical composition, most Alien species are likely to be sentient and intelligent. Intelligence is bound to be the great equalizer and the Universal Translator in our Universe. We may fail to recognize certain extragalactic races as life-forms but we are unlikely to mistake their intelligence for a naturally occurring phenomenon. We are equipped to know other sentient intelligent species regardless of how advanced and different they are - and they are equally fitted to acknowledge us as such.

Even so, should we ever encounter them, aliens are likely to strike as being childish and immature. Inevitably, they will find our planet strange. They will experience a learning curve (perhaps even a lengthy one). Similar to infants, they are likely to wander around, tumbling and gaping and clumsily reaching for objects, mute and possibly blinded by the light. They may be hampered by any number of things: gravity, the level of oxygen, radiation, and winds. Far from being a threat, at first they may require our assistance merely to survive the ordeal.

Argument Number 5: We are failing to communicate with Aliens

The hidden assumption underlying CETI/METI (Communication with ETI/Messaging to ETI) is that Aliens, like humans, are inclined to communicate. This may be untrue. The propensity for interpersonal communication (let alone the inter-species variety) may not be universal. Additionally, Aliens may not possess the same sense organs that we do (eyes) and may not be acquainted with our mathematics and geometry. Reality can be successfully described and captured by alternative mathematical systems and geometries.

Additionally, we often confuse complexity or orderliness with artificiality. As the example of quasars teaches us, not all regular or constant or strong or complex signals are artificial. Even the very use of language may be a uniquely human phenomenon - though most xenolinguists contest such exclusivity.

Moreover, as Wittgenstein observed, language is an essentially private affair: if a lion were to suddenly speak, we would not have understood it. Modern verificationist and referentialist linguistic theories seek to isolate the universals of language, so as to render all languages capable of translation - but they are still a long way off. Clarke's Third Law says that Alien civilizations well in advance of humanity may be deploying investigative methods and communicating in dialects undetectable even in principle by humans.

Argument Number 6: They are avoiding us

Advanced Alien civilizations may have found ways to circumvent the upper limit of the speed of light (for instance, by using wormholes). If they have and if UFO sightings are mere hoaxes and bunk (as is widely believed by most scientists), then we are back to Fermi's "where are they".

One possible answer is they are avoiding us because of our misconduct (example: the alleged destruction of the environment) or because of our traits (for instance, our innate belligerence). Or maybe the Earth is a galactic wildlife reserve or a zoo or a laboratory (the Zoo hypothesis) and the Aliens do not wish to contaminate us or subvert our natural development. This falsely assumes that all Alien civilizations operate in unison and under a single code (the Uniformity of Motive fallacy).

But how would they know to avoid contact with us? How would they know of our misdeeds and bad character?

Our earliest radio signals have traversed no more than 130 light years omnidirectionally. Out television emissions are even closer to home. What other source of information could Aliens have except our own self-incriminating transmissions? None. In other words, it is extremely unlikely that our reputation precedes us. Luckily for us, we are virtual unknowns.

As early as 1960, the implications of an encounter with an ETI were clear:

"Evidences of its existence might also be found in artifacts left on the moon or other planets. The consequences for attitudes and values are unpredictable, but would vary profoundly in different cultures and between groups within complex societies; a crucial factor would be the nature of the communication between us and the other beings. Whether or not earth would be inspired to an all-out space effort by such a discovery is moot: societies sure of their own place in the universe have disintegrated when confronted by a superior society, and others have survived even though changed. Clearly, the better we can come to understand

the factors involved in responding to such crises the better prepared we may be."

(Brookins Institute - Proposed Studies on the Implications of Peaceful Space Activities for Human Affairs, 1960)

Perhaps we should not be looking forward to the First Encounter. It may also be our last.

Return

Loving Gaze, Adulating Gaze

In the film "The Beaver", the character played by Mel Gibson suffers from depression. He latches on to a tattered puppet in the shape of a beaver and communicates exclusively through it. The Beaver is everything its ostensible master isn't: daring, creative, exuberant, omnipotent, and omniscient, gregarious, resourceful, charismatic, and charming; a good father, good CEO, and good company all around. In short: The Beaver is the reification of the protagonist's False Self.

When his wife (Jodi Foster) confronts him, having exposed his confabulations and the need to let go of the contraption, The Beaver rages at her and asserts its superiority, invincibility, and brilliance. The depressive Walter – the True Self - is derided by The Beaver as a dysfunctional wreck, utterly dependent on the former's ministrations and the interference it runs on his behalf. The film ends unrealistically with Walter mutilating his body – literally - in order to rid himself of the domineering and all-pervasive appendage. "Unrealistically" because narcissists never succeed in resuscitating their dilapidated and crushed True Self. The narcissist *IS* his False Self: in real life, Walter should have been devoured and consumed by The Beaver – but then we would not have had a typical, syrupy Happy Ending, now, would we?

Both the True Self and the False Self depend on the gaze of others. The False Self relies on adulation and attention – narcissistic supply – for the maintenance of the precarious, confabulated, fantastic, grandiose, and counterfactual narrative that is the narcissist's persona, his public face. Without a constant flow of such high-quality input and feedback, without the **adulating gaze**, the narcissist crumbles like a house of ephemeral cards and resorts to a variety of dysfunctional, self-destructive, and self-defeating behaviors and defense mechanisms.

Similarly and equally, the True Self needs a **loving gaze** to sustain itself. Another person's love serves two purposes: it confirms the existence of the True Self as a lovable object and thus lays the groundwork and facilitates the necessary and sufficient conditions for self-love; and it allows the True Self to perceive the existence of a "safe", loving, and holding other. Such insight is at the very foundation of empathy.

Do the False and True Selves ever fight it out, David vs. Goliath, Good vs. Evil, The Beaver vs. Walter?

Alas, they never do. The False Self is concocted by the narcissist to fend off hurt. It is a perfect, impenetrable, impermeable shield, a cocoon; it rewards the narcissist by flooding him with warm, fuzzy, exhilarating feelings; and it sustains the narcissist's delusions and fantasies. The False Self is the narcissist's dreams come true. In other words: as far as the narcissist is concerned, the False Self is adaptive and functional. The narcissist is emotionally invested in the False Self and he despises the True Self for having failed to cope with the exigencies and vicissitudes of the narcissist's life.

Return

The Malignant Optimism of the Abused

The profoundly disturbing film "We Need to Talk about Kevin" is told from the mother's point of view. Kevin is a maladjusted kid with a conduct disorder who blooms into a full-fledged blood-curdling psychopath in his teens. His mother is one of his victims. Kevin ends up killing his entire family (his mother ends up being the sole survivor and witness to the massacre) as well as numerous schoolmates before he is apprehended.

The film ends with his mother, now reduced to a dysfunctional shell and shadow of her former self, visiting him in prison on a regular basis and hugging him for good measure.

Some victims never learn. You hear them saying:

"It is true that he is a chauvinistic narcissist and that his behaviour is unacceptable and repulsive. But all he needs is a little love and he will be straightened out. I will rescue him from his misery and misfortune. I will give him the love that he lacked as a child. Then his narcissism will vanish and we will live happily ever after."

I often come across sad examples of the powers of self-delusion that the narcissist provokes in his victims. It is what I call "malignant optimism". People refuse to believe that some questions are unsolvable, some diseases incurable, some disasters inevitable. They see a sign of hope in every fluctuation. They read meaning and patterns into every random occurrence, utterance, or slip. They are deceived by their own pressing need to believe in the ultimate victory of good over evil, health over sickness, order over disorder. Life appears otherwise so meaningless, so unjust and so arbitrary...

So, they impose upon it a design, progress, aims, and paths. This is magical thinking.

"If only he tried hard enough", "If he only really wanted to heal", "If only we found the right therapy", "If only his defences were down", "There MUST be something good and worthy under the hideous facade", "NO ONE can be that evil and destructive", "He must have meant it differently" "God, or a higher being, or the spirit, or the soul is the solution and the answer to our prayers".

The Pollyanna defences of the abused are aimed against the emerging and horrible understanding that humans are specks of dust in a totally indifferent universe, the playthings of evil and sadistic forces, of which the narcissist is one - as well as against the unbearable realization that their pain means nothing to anyone but themselves. Nothing whatsoever. It has all been in vain.

The narcissist holds such thinking in barely undisguised contempt. To him, it is a sign of weakness, the scent of prey, a gaping vulnerability. He uses and abuses this human need for order, good, and meaning - as he uses and abuses all other human needs. Gullibility, selective blindness, malignant optimism - these are the weapons of the beast. And the abused are hard at work to provide it with its arsenal.

Return

The Disruptive Engine

Innovation and the Capitalistic Dream

The film "The Artist" describes the waning career of a megastar of the era of silent movies when he refuses to make the transition into the epoch of "talkies" (films with sound.) He mocks the innovation and then challenges it by producing a lavish production of yet another silent epic. His inevitable downfall follows. He is reduced to pawning and auctioning off his few remaining belongings.

In the biological realms, genetic mutations ensure that the repertory of responses to constantly varying circumstances is always fresh and never depleted. Not so in the world of business where success often spells death and doom and it is failure that spurs innovation. Indeed, the successful firms of yesteryear are often forgotten: no one can name the three dominant horse whip manufacturers in the 19th century, for instance. Silent era film stars are also not household names.

Business success is due to an appealing or groundbreaking product (which generates its own market and demand), an efficient process, or a fortuitous and serendipitous set of events coupled with emerging needs. The overwhelming advantage of the first-mover guarantees that competitors (mostly imitators) are left far behind. Brand recognition, customer loyalty and intellectual property protections pose often insurmountable barriers to entry. This forces newcomers to innovate or perish.

Faced with challengers, monopolies and duopolies, or even oligopolies retrench. Why don't these companies counter-innovate? Because they are emotionally-invested in their cash cows, their current best-selling offerings, and the managerial-organizational structures and processes they gave rise to. Fears of rocking the boat and of the unknown mingle with the haughtiness of the well-to-do and the inertia and anti-entrepreneurial culture that are the hallmarks of big business. Finally, the institutional knowledge of successful firms and their skills set are skewed in favour of existing products and processes. Lurking in the back of everyone's mind, from the upper echelons of management to the lowliest menial labourer is the question: "As long as the money keeps pouring in – why bother to innovate? Why take chances?"

Indeed, innovation is an entirely modern concept. Up to the 19th century, innovators were penalized for daring to upset the proverbial applecart. Imitators, conservatives, and traditionalists were richly rewarded. The culture of successful companies tends to resemble this period of pre-Industrial Revolution.

War and money confer an evolutionary advantage on Mankind by spurring innovation: hence their ubiquity. Attempts to foster creativity and genius via state largesse, the education system, and bolstering entrepreneurship pale in comparison to the accomplishments wrought on by belligerence and cupidity.

On 18 June, 2002 business people across the UK took part in Living Innovation 2002. The extravaganza included a national broadcast linkup from the Eden Project in Cornwall and satellite-televised interviews with successful innovators.

Innovation occurs even in the most backward societies and in the hardest of times. It is thus, too often, taken for granted. But the intensity, extent, and practicality of innovation can be fine-tuned. Appropriate policies, the right environment, incentives, functional and risk seeking capital markets, or a skillful and committed Diaspora - can all enhance and channel innovation.

The wrong cultural context, discouraging social mores, xenophobia, a paranoid set of mind, isolation from international trade and FDI, lack of fiscal incentives, a small domestic or regional market, a conservative ethos, risk aversion, or a well-ingrained fear of disgracing failure - all tend to stifle innovation.

Product Development Units in banks, insurers, brokerage houses, and other financial intermediaries churn out groundbreaking financial instruments regularly. Governments - from the United Kingdom to New Zealand - set up "innovation teams or units" to foster innovation and support it. Canada's is more than two decades old.

In the first decade of the 21st century, the European Commission has floated a new program dubbed INNOVATION and aimed at the promotion of innovation and encouragement of SME participation. Its goals are:

- "(The) promotion of an environment favourable to innovation and the absorption of new technologies by enterprises;
- Stimulation of a European open area for the diffusion of technologies and knowledge;
- Supply of this area with appropriate technologies."

But all these worthy efforts ignore what James O'Toole called in "Leading Change" - "the ideology of comfort and the tyranny of custom." The much quoted Austrian economist, Joseph Schumpeter coined the phrase "creative destruction". Together with its twin - "disruptive technologies" - it came to be the mantra of the now defunct "New Economy".

Schumpeter seemed to have captured the unsettling nature of innovation - unpredictable, unknown, unruly, troublesome, and ominous. Innovation often changes the inner dynamics of organizations and their internal power structure. It poses new demands on scarce resources. It provokes resistance and unrest. If mismanaged - it can spell doom rather than boom.

Satkar Gidda, Sales and Marketing Director for SiebertHead, a large UK packaging design house, was quoted in "The Financial Times" as saying:

"Every new product or pack concept is researched to death nowadays - and many great ideas are thrown out simply because a group of consumers is suspicious of anything that sounds new ... Conservatism among the buying public, twinned with a generation of marketing directors who won't take a chance on something that breaks new ground, is leading to super-markets and car showrooms full of me-too products, line extensions and minor product tweaks."

Yet, the truth is that no one knows why people innovate. The process of innovation has never been studied thoroughly - nor are the effects of innovation fully understood.

In a new tome titled "The Free-Market Innovation Machine", William Baumol of Princeton University claims that only capitalism guarantees growth through a steady flow of innovation:

"... Innovative activity-which in other types of economy is fortuitous and optional-becomes mandatory, a life-and-death matter for the firm."

Capitalism makes sure that innovators are rewarded for their time and skills. Property rights are enshrined in enforceable contracts. In non-capitalist societies, people are busy inventing ways to survive or circumvent the system, create monopolies, or engage in crime.

But Baumol fails to sufficiently account for the different levels of innovation in capitalistic countries. Why are inventors in America more productive than their French or British counterparts - at least judging by the number of patents they get issued? And why did innovation blossom in the USSR throughout its existence?

Perhaps because oligopolies are more common in the US than they are elsewhere. Baumol suggests that oligopolies use their excess rent - i.e., profits which exceed perfect competition takings - to innovate and thus to differentiate their products. Still, oligopolistic behavior does not sit well with another of Baumol's observations: that innovators tend to maximize their returns by sharing their technology and licensing it to more efficient and profitable manufacturers. Nor can one square this propensity to share with the ever more stringent and expansive intellectual property laws that afflict many rich countries nowadays.

Very few inventions have forced "established companies from their dominant market positions" as the "The Economist" put it recently. Moreover, most novelties are spawned by established companies. The single, tortured, and misunderstood inventor working on a shoestring budget in his garage - is a mythical relic of 18th century Romanticism.

More often, innovation is systematically and methodically pursued by teams of scientists and researchers in the labs of mega-corporations and endowed academic institutions. Governments - and, more particularly the defense establishment - finance most of this brainstorming. the Internet was invented by DARPA - a Department of Defense agency - and not by libertarian intellectuals.

A report compiled by PricewaterhouseCoopers from interviews with 800 CEO's in the UK, France, Germany, Spain, Australia, Japan and the US and titled "Innovation and Growth: A Global Perspective" included the following findings:

"High-performing companies - those that generate annual total shareholder returns in excess of 37 percent and have seen consistent revenue growth over the last five years - average 61 percent of their turnover from new products and services. For low performers, only 26 percent of turnover comes from new products and services."

Most of the respondents attributed the need to innovate to increasing pressures to brand and differentiate exerted by the advent of e-business and globalization. Yet a full three quarters admitted to being entirely unprepared for the new challenges.

Two good places to study routine innovation are the design studio and the financial markets.

Tom Kelly, brother of founder David Kelly, studies, in "The Art of Innovation", the history of some of the greater inventions to have been incubated in IDEO, a prominent California-based design firm dubbed "Innovation U." by Fortune Magazine. These include the computer mouse, the instant camera, and the PDA. The secret of success seems to consist of keenly observing what people miss most when they work and play.

Robert Morris, an Amazon reviewer, sums up IDEO's creative process:

- Understand the market, the client, the technology, and the perceived constraints on the given problem;
- Observe real people in real-life situations;
- Literally visualize new-to-the- world concepts AND the customers who will use them;
- Evaluate and refine the prototypes in a series of quick iterations;
- And finally, implement the new concept for commercialization.

This methodology is a hybrid between the lone-inventor and the faceless corporate R&D team. An entirely different process of innovation characterizes the financial markets. Jacob Goldenberg and David Mazursky postulated the existence of Creativity Templates. Once systematically applied to existing products, these lead to innovation.

Financial innovation is methodical and product-centric. The resulting trade in pioneering products, such as all manner of derivatives, has expanded 20-fold between 1986 and 1999, when annual trading volume exceeded 13 trillion dollar.

Swiss Re Economic Research and Consulting had this to say in its study, Sigma 3/2001:

"Three types of factors drive financial innovation: demand, supply, and taxes and regulation. Demand driven innovation occurs in response to the desire of companies to protect themselves from market risks ... Supply side factors ... include improvements in technology and heightened competition among financial service firms. Other financial innovation occurs as a rational response to taxes and regulation, as firms seek to minimize the cost that these impose."

Financial innovation is closely related to breakthroughs in information technology. Both markets are founded on the manipulation of symbols and coded concepts. The dynamic of these markets is self-reinforcing. Faster computers with more massive storage, speedier data transfer ("pipeline"), and networking capabilities - give rise to all forms of advances - from math-rich derivatives contracts to distributed computing. These, in turn, drive software companies, creators of content, financial engineers, scientists, and inventors to a heightened complexity of thinking. It is a virtuous cycle in which innovation generates the very tools that facilitate further innovation.

The eminent American economist Robert Merton - quoted in Sigma 3/2001 - described in the Winter 1992 issue of the "Journal of Applied Corporate Finance" the various phases of the market-buttressed spiral of financial innovation thus:

1. "In the first stage ... there is a proliferation of standardised securities such as futures. These securities make possible the creation of custom-designed financial products ...
2. In the second stage, volume in the new market expands as financial intermediaries trade to hedge their market exposures.
3. The increased trading volume in turn reduces financial transaction costs and thereby makes further implementation of new products and trading strategies possible, which leads to still more volume.
4. The success of these trading markets then encourages investments in creating additional markets, and the financial system spirals towards the theoretical limit of zero transaction costs and dynamically complete markets."

Financial innovation is not adjuvant. Innovation is useless without finance - whether in the form of equity or debt. Schumpeter himself gave equal weight to new forms of "credit creation" which invariably accompanied each technological "paradigm shift". In the absence of stock options and venture capital - there would have been no Microsoft or Intel.

It would seem that both management gurus and ivory tower academics agree that innovation - technological and financial - is an inseparable part of competition. Tom Peters put it succinctly in "The Circle of Innovation" when he wrote: "Innovate or die". James Morse, a management consultant, rendered, in the same tome, the same lesson more verbosely: "The only sustainable competitive advantage comes from out-innovating the competition."

The OECD published a study titled "Productivity and Innovation". It summarizes the orthodoxy, first formulated by Nobel prizewinner Robert Solow from MIT almost five decades ago:

"A substantial part of economic growth cannot be explained by increased utilisation of capital and labour. This part of growth, commonly labelled 'multi-factor productivity', represents improvements in the efficiency of production. It is usually seen as the result of innovation by best-practice firms, technological catch-up by other firms, and reallocation of resources across firms and industries."

The study analyzed the entire OECD area. It concluded, unsurprisingly, that easing regulatory restrictions enhances productivity and that policies that favor competition spur innovation. They do so by making it easier to adjust the factors of production and by facilitating the entrance of new firms - mainly in rapidly evolving industries.

Pro-competition policies stimulate increases in efficiency and product diversification. They help shift output to innovative industries. More unconventionally, as the report diplomatically put it: "The effects on innovation of easing job protection are complex" and "Excessive intellectual property rights protection may hinder the development of new processes and products."

As expected, the study found that productivity performance varies across countries reflecting their ability to reach and then shift the technological frontier - a direct outcome of aggregate innovative effort.

Yet, innovation may be curbed by even more all-pervasive and pernicious problems. "The Economist" posed a question to its readers in the December 2001 issue of its Technology Quarterly:

Was *"technology losing its knack of being able to invent a host of solutions for any given problem ... (and) as a corollary, (was) innovation ... running out of new ideas to exploit."*

These worrying trends were attributed to *"the soaring cost of developing high-tech products ... as only one of the reasons why technological choice is on the wane, as one or two firms emerge as the sole suppliers. The trend towards globalisation-of markets as much as manufacturing-was seen as another cause of this loss of engineering diversity ... (as was the) the widespread use of safety standards that emphasise detailed design specifications instead of setting minimum performance requirements for designers to achieve any way they wish.*

Then there was the commoditisation of technology brought on largely by the cross-licensing and patent-trading between rival firms, which more or less guarantees that many of their products are essentially the same ... (Another innovation-inhibiting problem is that) increasing knowledge was leading to increasing specialisation - with little or no cross- communication between experts in different fields ...

... Maturing technology can quickly become de-skilled as automated tools get developed so designers can harness the technology's power without having to understand its inner workings. The more that happens, the more engineers closest to the technology become incapable of contributing improvements to it. And without such user input, a technology can quickly ossify."

The readers overwhelmingly rejected these contentions. The rate of innovation, they asserted, has actually accelerated with wider spread education and more efficient weeding-out of unfit solutions by the marketplace. *"... Technology in the 21st century is going to be less about discovering new phenomena and more about putting known things together with greater imagination and efficiency."*

Many cited the S-curve to illuminate the current respite. Innovation is followed by selection, improvement of the surviving models, shake-out among competing suppliers, and convergence on a single solution. Information technology has matured - but new S-curves are nascent: nanotechnology, quantum computing, proteomics, neuro-silicates, and machine intelligence.

Recent innovations have spawned two crucial ethical debates, though with accentuated pragmatic aspects. The first is "open source-free access" versus proprietary technology and the second revolves around the role of technological progress in re-defining relationships between stakeholders.

Both issues are related to the inadvertent re-engineering of the corporation. Modern technology helped streamline firms by removing layers of paper-shuffling management.

It placed great power in the hands of the end-user, be it an executive, a household, or an individual. It reversed the trends of centralization and hierarchical stratification wrought by the Industrial Revolution. From microprocessor to micropower - an enormous centrifugal shift is underway. Power percolates back to the people.

Thus, the relationships between user and supplier, customer and company, shareholder and manager, medium and consumer - are being radically reshaped. In an intriguing spin on this theme, Michael Cox and Richard Alm argue in their book "Myths of Rich and Poor - Why We are Better off than We Think" that income inequality actually engenders innovation. The rich and corporate clients pay exorbitant prices for prototypes and new products, thus cross-subsidising development costs for the poorer majority.

Yet the poor are malcontent. They want equal access to new products. One way of securing it is by having the poor develop the products and then disseminate them free of charge. The development effort is done collectively, by volunteers. Open source software, such as the Linux operating system is an example as is the Open Directory Project which competed with the commercial Yahoo! Directory.

The UNDP's Human Development Report 2001 titled "Making new technologies work for human development" is unequivocal. Innovation and access to technologies are the keys to poverty-reduction through sustained growth. Technology helps reduce mortality rates, disease, and hunger among the destitute.

"The Economist" carried last December the story of the agricultural technologist Richard Jefferson who helps "local plant breeders and growers develop the foods they think best ... CAMBIA (the institute he founded) has resisted the lure of exclusive licences and shareholder investment, because it wants its work to be freely available and widely used". This may well foretell the shape of things to come.

Return

What to Expect When You Are Expecting

Modern pop culture bombards us with gender stereotypes, which by now have become truisms: women are always sensitive, misunderstood, in touch with their emotions and neglected; men are commitment-phobic, confused, narcissistic, hypersexed, and hell-bent on frustrating the opposite number.

It was, therefore, refreshing to watch the four female protagonists of the film "What to Expect When You Are Expecting" reduce these caricatures to smithereens. The womenfolk in the film are self-centered, dread intimacy and commitment, two of them are workaholics, and all four are rank narcissists.

The men in this otherwise middling movie are romantic, in touch with their emotions, committed, and largely selfless. The only exception is the dysfunctional father of one of them, a throwback to the 1960s when men were still machos and sex meant everything. His youthful wife makes up for his shortcomings, though: she is clear-headed, no-nonsense, determined, sharp-witted, and a strict disciplinarian when needed. But this incongruous couple is the only exception to an otherwise coherent message: men have matured, women should get their act together.

The women are the ones who - not so secretly - abhor the thought of what bearing children would do to their bodies and to their lives (in this order.) The men encourage them to be fruitful and multiply as the ultimate fad in self-fulfillment and self-gratification.

Another striking feature of this film is the fact that none of the women, despite being all over the place, feels the need to seek advice. They live alone and cope in solitude: gone are the tips-dispensing mother; the supportive female soulmate; The effeminate or gay male friend; the recurring old flame; the motherly colleague or avuncular co-worker. It's every woman for herself now. And they are botching the job, says the film, as thoroughly as men ever did.

The Death of Traditional Sex in a Unisex World

Traditional sex – the heady cocktail of lust and emotional bonding - is all but dead. In a culture of casual, almost anonymous hookups, suppressing attendant emerging emotions is the bon ton and women and men drift apart, zerovalent atoms in an ever-shifting, kaleidoscopic world, separated by a yawning expectations gap, their virtual isolation aided and abetted by technologies, collectively misnomered "social media".

It is increasingly more difficult to both find a mate and keep him or her. One fifth of all American couples are sexless. In Japan, about half of all adolescents are schizoid and prefer technological gadgets to flesh-and-blood peers. A quarter of all males in Britain would rather watch the telly or bar crawl with their friends than garner carnal pleasure. People everywhere increasingly rely on Internet porn and auto-erotic stimulation to relieve themselves. Sex has become the sordid equivalent of other excretory bodily functions, best pursued in solitude.

At the root of this upheaval is the ill-thought and violent subversion of received gender roles. Women sought to become not only equal to men, but identical to them.

Rather than encourage a peaceful evolution, they embarked on a series of shattering and disorienting gender wars with men as the demonized enemy. Attempting assertiveness, women found aggression.

Relationships have become virulent battlefields and the zero testing grounds of a brave, new world. No wonder men find women bafflingly masculine and unattractive. They recoil from commitment and bonding because the rules of engagement are fuzzy, the resources required depleting, the rewards scanty, and the risks – pecuniary and emotional – devastating. Birth rates have plunged well below the replacement rate in most industrialized societies: childrearing requires stable arrangements with reasonable prognoses of functional health and longevity.

In short: the typical, chauvinistic male still wants to get married to his grandmother and his narcissistic female counterparty wishes to live happily ever after with a penile reflection of herself. The differences in expectations lead to discrepancies in performance which are all but unbridgeable and irreconcilable. Breakup rates are unprecedented in human history. The lucrative business of divorce is no longer frowned upon and is facilitated by lenient legislation and a veritable cornucopia of institutions. The proliferation of models of pairing and cohabitation is proof positive that the system is broken: it's every man for himself now. Society is even more clueless and impotent than the individuals it is ostensibly comprised of and, therefore, can provide no normative guidance.

People react to this massive rupture in various ways: some abstain from or renounce sex altogether; a few experiment with bi- or homosexuality; others immerse themselves in cybersex in its multifarious forms; many choose one night stands and random encounters rendered riskless by contraceptives and made widely available via modern transportation and telecommunication. Opportunities for all the above abound and, socially well-tolerated, recreational, non-committal, and emotionless sex is on the rise.

But the roots of the crumbling alliance between men and women go deeper and further in time. Long before divorce became a social norm, men and women grew into two disparate, incompatible, and warring subspecies. Traditionalist, conservative, and religious societies put in place behavioural safeguards against the inevitable wrenching torsion that monogamy entailed: no premarital sex (virginity); no multiple intimate partners; no cohabitation prior to tying the knot; no mobility, or equal rights for women; no mixing of the genders. We now know that each of these habits does, indeed, increase the chances for an ultimate divorce. As Jonathan Franzen elucidates in his literary masterpieces, it boils down to a choice between personal freedoms and the stability of the family: the former decisively preclude the latter.

During the 17th, 18th, and 19th centuries, discreet affairs were an institution of marriage: sexual gratification and emotional intimacy were outsourced while all other domestic functions were shared in partnership. The Industrial Revolution, the Victorian Age, the backlash of the sexual revolution, belligerent feminism, and the advent of socially-atomizing and gender-equalizing transportation, information processing, and telecommunication technologies led inexorably to the hollowing out of family and hearth.

In a civilization centred on brainpower, Men have lost the relative edge that brawn used to provide. Monogamy is increasingly considered as past its expiry date: a historical aberration that reflects the economic and political realities of bygone eras. Moreover: the incidence of lifelong, childfree (or childless) singlehood has skyrocketed as people hope for their potential or actual relationship-partners to provide for all their sexual, emotional, social, and economic needs – and then get sorely disappointed when they fail to meet these highly unrealistic expectations.

In an age of economic self-sufficiency, electronic entertainment, and self-gratification, the art of compromise in relationships is gone. Single motherhood (sometimes via IVF, with no identifiable partner involved) has become the norm in many countries. Even within marriages or committed relationships, solitary pursuits, such as separate vacations, or "girls'/boy' nights out" have become the norm.

The 20th century was a monument to male fatuity: wars and ideologies almost decimated the species. Forced to acquire masculine skills and fill men's shoes in factories and fields, women discovered militant self-autonomy, the superfluousness of men, and the untenability of the male claims to superiority over them.

In an age of malignant individualism, bordering on narcissism, men and women alike put themselves, their fantasies, and their needs first, all else – family included – be damned. And with 5 decades of uninterrupted prosperity, birth control, and feminism/ women's lib most of the female denizens of the West have acquired the financial wherewithal to realize their dreams at the expense and to the detriment of collectives they ostensibly belong to (such as the nuclear family.) Feminism is a movement focused on negatives (obliterating women's age-old bondage) but it offers few constructive ideas regarding women's new roles. By casting men as the enemy, it also failed to educate them and convert them into useful allies.

Owing to the dramatic doubling of life expectancy, modern marriages seem to go through three phases: infatuation (honeymoon); procreation-accumulation (of assets, children, and shared experiences); and exhaustion-outsourcing (bonding with new emotional and sexual partners for rejuvenation or the fulfilment of long-repressed fantasies, needs, and wishes.) Divorces and breakups occur mostly at the seams, the periods of transition between these phases and especially between the stages of accumulation-procreation and exhaustion-outsourcing. This is where family units break down.

With marriage on the decline and infidelity on the rise, the reasonable solution would be swinging (swapping sexual partners) or polyamory (households with multiple partners of both genders all of whom are committed to one another for the long haul, romantically-involved, sexually-shared, and economically united.) Alas, while a perfectly rational development of the traditional marriage and one that is best-suited to modernity, it is an emotionally unstable setup, what with romantic jealousy ineluctably rearing its ugly head. Very few people are emotionally capable of sharing their life-partner with others.

The question is not why there are so many divorces, but why so few. Surely, serial monogamy is far better, fairer, and more humane than adultery? Couples stay together and tolerate straying owing to inertia; financial or emotional dependence; insecurity (lack of self-confidence or low self-esteem); fear of the unknown and the tedium of dating. Some couples persevere owing to religious conviction of for the sake of appearances. Yet others make a smooth transition to an alternative lifestyle (polyamory, swinging, or consensual adultery).

Indeed, what has changed is not the incidence of adultery, even among women. There are good grounds to assume that it has remained the same throughout human history. The phenomenon - quantitatively and qualitatively - has always been the same, merely underreported. What have changed are the social acceptability of extramarital sex both before and during marriage and the ease of obtaining divorce. People discuss adultery openly where before it was a taboo topic.

Another new development may be the rise of "selfish affairs" among women younger than 35 who are used to multiple sexual partners. "Selfish affairs" are acts of recreational adultery whose sole purpose is to satisfy sexual curiosity and the need for romantic diversity. The emotional component in these usually short-term affairs (one-night stands and the like) is muted. Among women older than 60, adultery has become the accepted way of seeking emotional connection and intimacy outside the marital bond. These are "outsourcing affairs."

The ancient institution of monogamous marriage is ill-suited to the exigencies of modern Western civilization. People of both genders live and work longer (which renders monogamy impracticable); travel far and away frequently; and are exposed to tempting romantic alternatives via social networking and in various workplace and social settings.

Thus, even as social monogamy and pair commitment and bonding are still largely intact and more condoned than ever and even as infidelity is fervently condemned, sexual exclusivity (mislabelled "sexual monogamy") is declining, especially among the young and the old. Monogamy is becoming one alternative among many lifestyles and marriage only one relationship among a few (sometimes, not even a privileged or unique relationship, as it competes for time and resources with work, same-sex friends, friends with benefits, and opposite-sex friends.)

The contractual aspects of marriage are more pronounced than ever with everything on the table: from extramarital sex (allowed or not) to pre-nuptial agreements. The commodification and preponderance of sex – premarital and extramarital - robbed it of its function as a conduit of specialness and intimacy and since childrearing is largely avoided (natality rates are precipitously plummeting everywhere) or outsourced, the family has lost both its raison d'être and its nature as the venue for exclusive sexual and emotional interactions between adults.

Professed values and prevailing social mores and institutions have yet to catch up to this emerging multifarious reality. The consequences of these discrepancies are disastrous: about 40-50% of all first-time marriages end in divorce and the percentage is much higher for second and third attempts at connubial bliss. Open communication about one's sexual needs is tantamount to self-ruination as one's partner is likely to reflexively initiate a divorce. Dishonesty and cheating are definitely the rational choices in such an unforgiving and punitive environment.

Indeed, most surviving marriages have to do with perpetuating the partners' convenience, their access to commonly-owned assets and future streams of income, and the welfare of third parties, most notably their kids. Erstwhile sexual exclusivity often degenerates into celibacy or abstinence on the one hand – or parallel lives with multiple sexual and emotional partners on the other hand.

One night stands for both genders are usually opportunistic. Extra-pair affairs are self-limiting, as emotional involvement and sexual attraction wane over time. Infidelity is, therefore, much less of a threat to the longevity of a dedicated couple than it is made out to be. Most of the damage is caused by culturally-conditioned, albeit deeply and traumatically felt, reactions to conduct that is almost universally decried as deceitful, dishonest, and in breach of vows and promises.

Until recently, couples formed around promises of emotional exclusivity and sexual fidelity, uniqueness in each other's mind and life, and (more common until the 1940s) virginity. Marriage was also a partnership:

economic, or related to childrearing, or companionship. It was based on the partners' past and background and geared towards a shared future.

Nowadays, couples coalesce around the twin undertakings of continuity ("I will ALWAYS be there for you") and availability ("I will always BE there for you.") Issues of exclusivity, uniqueness, and virginity have been relegated to the back-burner. It is no longer practical to demand of one's spouse to have nothing to do with the opposite sex, not to spend the bulk of his or her time outside the marriage, not to take separate vacations, and, more generally, to be joined at the hip. Affairs, for instance – both emotional and sexual – are sad certainties in the life of every couple.

Members of the couple are supposed to make themselves continuously available to each other and to provide emotional sustenance and support in an atmosphere of sharing, companionship, and friendship. All the traditional functions of the family can now be – and often are – outsourced, including even sex and emotional intimacy. But, contrary to marriage, outsourcing is frequently haphazard and unpredictable, dependent as it is on outsiders who are committed elsewhere as well. Hence the relative durability of marriage, in its conservative and less-conventional forms alike: it is a convenient and highly practicable arrangement.

Divorce or other forms of marital breakup are not new phenomena. But their precipitants have undergone a revolutionary shift. In the past, families fell apart owing to a breach of exclusivity, mainly in the forms of emotional or sexual infidelity; a deficiency of uniqueness and primacy: divorced women, for instance, were considered "damaged goods" because they used to "belong" to another man and, therefore, could offer neither primacy nor uniqueness; or an egregious violation of the terms of partnership (for example: sloth, dysfunctional childrearing, infertility).

Nowadays, intimate partners bail out when the continuous availability of their significant others is disrupted: sexually, emotionally, or as friends and companions. Marriages are about the present and are being put to the test on a daily basis. Partners who are dissatisfied opt out and team up with other, more promising providers. Children are serially reared by multiple parents and in multiple households.

Sex and Gender

"One is not born, but rather becomes, a woman."

Simone de Beauvoir, The Second Sex (1949)

With same-sex marriage becoming a legal reality throughout the world, many more children are going to be raised by homosexual (gay and lesbian) parents, or even by transgendered or transsexual ones. How is this going to affect the child's masculinity or femininity?

Is being a gay man less manly than being a heterosexual one? Is a woman who is the outcome of a sex change operation less feminine than her natural-born sisters? In which sense is a "virile" lesbian less of a man than an effeminate heterosexual or homosexual man? And how should we classify and treat bisexuals and asexuals?

What about modern she-breadwinners? All those feminist women in traditional male positions who are as sexually aggressive as men and prone to the same varieties of misconduct (e.g., cheating on their spouses)? Are they less womanly? And are their stay-at-home-dad partners not men enough? How are sex preferences related to gender differentiation? And if one's sex and genitalia can be chosen and altered at will – why not one's gender, regardless of one's natural equipment? Can we decouple gender roles from sexual functions and endowments?

Aren't the feminist-liberal-emancipated woman and her responsive, transformed male partner as moulded by specific social norms and narratives as their more traditional and conservative counterparts? And when men adapted to the demands of the "new", post-modernist woman – were they not then rebuffed by that very same female as emasculated and unmanly? What is the source of this gender chaos? Why do people act "modern" while, at heart, they still hark back to erstwhile mores and ethos?

In nature, male and female are distinct. She-elephants are gregarious, he-elephants solitary. Male zebra finches are loquacious - the females mute. Female green spoon worms are 200,000 times larger than their male mates. These striking differences are biological - yet they lead to differentiation in social roles and skill acquisition.

Alan Pease, author of a book titled "Why Men Don't Listen and Women Can't Read Maps", believes that women are spatially-challenged compared to men. The British firm, Admiral Insurance, conducted a study of half a million claims. They found that "women were almost twice as likely as men to have a collision in a car park, 23 percent more likely to hit a stationary car, and 15 percent more likely to reverse into another vehicle" (Reuters).

Yet gender "differences" are often the outcomes of bad scholarship. Consider Admiral Insurance's data. As Britain's Automobile Association (AA) correctly pointed out - women drivers tend to make more short journeys around towns and shopping centers and these involve frequent parking. Hence their ubiquity in certain kinds of claims. Regarding women's alleged spatial deficiency, in Britain, girls have been outperforming boys in scholastic aptitude tests - including geometry and maths - since 1988.

In an Op-Ed published by the New York Times on January 23, 2005, Olivia Judson cited this example

"Beliefs that men are intrinsically better at this or that have repeatedly led to discrimination and prejudice, and then they've been proved to be nonsense. Women were thought not to be world-class musicians. But when American symphony orchestras introduced blind auditions in the 1970's - the musician plays behind a screen so that his or her gender is invisible to those listening - the number of women offered jobs in professional orchestras increased. Similarly, in science, studies of the ways that grant applications are evaluated have shown that women are more likely to get financing when those reading the applications do not know the sex of the applicant."

On the other wing of the divide, Anthony Clare, a British psychiatrist and author of "On Men" wrote:

"At the beginning of the 21st century it is difficult to avoid the conclusion that men are in serious trouble. Throughout the world, developed and developing, antisocial behavior is essentially male. Violence, sexual abuse of children, illicit drug use, alcohol misuse, gambling, all are overwhelmingly male activities. The courts and prisons bulge with men. When it comes to aggression, delinquent behavior, risk taking and social mayhem, men win gold."

Men also mature later, die earlier, are more susceptible to infections and most types of cancer, are more likely to be dyslexic, to suffer from a host of mental health disorders, such as Attention Deficit Hyperactivity Disorder (ADHD), and to commit suicide.

In her book, "Stiffed: The Betrayal of the American Man", Susan Faludi describes a crisis of masculinity following the breakdown of manhood models and work and family structures in the last five decades. In the film "Boys don't Cry", a teenage girl binds her breasts and acts the male in a caricatured relish of stereotypes of virility. Being a man is merely a state of mind, the movie implies.

But what does it really mean to be a "male" or a "female"? Are gender identity and sexual preferences genetically determined? Can they be reduced to one's sex? Or are they amalgams of biological, social, and psychological factors in constant interaction? Are they immutable lifelong features or dynamically evolving frames of self-reference?

In rural northern Albania, until recently, in families with no male heir, women could choose to forego sex and childbearing, alter their external appearance and "become" men and the patriarchs of their clans, with all the attendant rights and obligations.

In the aforementioned New York Times Op-Ed, Olivia Judson opines:

"Many sex differences are not, therefore, the result of his having one gene while she has another. Rather, they are attributable to the way particular genes behave when they find themselves in him instead of her. The magnificent difference between male and female green spoon worms, for example, has nothing to do with their having different genes: each green spoon worm larva could go either way. Which sex it becomes depends on whether it meets a female during its first three weeks of life. If it meets a female, it becomes male and prepares to regurgitate; if it doesn't, it becomes female and settles into a crack on the sea floor."

Yet, certain traits attributed to one's sex are surely better accounted for by the demands of one's environment, by cultural factors, the process of socialization, gender roles, and what George Devereux called "ethnopsychiatry" in "Basic Problems of Ethnopsychiatry" (University of Chicago Press, 1980). He suggested to divide the unconscious into the id (the part that was always instinctual and unconscious) and the "ethnic unconscious" (repressed material that was once conscious). The latter is mostly molded by prevailing cultural mores and includes all our defense mechanisms and most of the superego.

So, how can we tell whether our sexual role is mostly in our blood or in our brains?

The scrutiny of borderline cases of human sexuality - notably the transgendered or intersexed - can yield clues as to the distribution and relative weights of biological, social, and psychological determinants of gender identity formation.

The results of a study conducted by Uwe Hartmann, Hinnerk Becker, and Claudia Rueffer-Hesse in 1997 and titled "Self and Gender: Narcissistic Pathology and Personality Factors in Gender Dysphoric Patients", published in the "International Journal of Transgenderism", "indicate significant psychopathological aspects and narcissistic dysregulation in a substantial proportion of patients." Are these "psychopathological aspects" merely reactions to underlying physiological realities and changes? Could social ostracism and labeling have induced them in the "patients"?

The authors conclude:

"The cumulative evidence of our study ... is consistent with the view that gender dysphoria is a disorder of the sense of self as has been proposed by Beitel (1985) or Pfäfflin (1993). The central problem in our patients is about identity and the self in general and the transsexual wish seems to be an attempt at reassuring and stabilizing the self-coherence which in turn can lead to a further destabilization if the self is already too fragile. In this view the body is instrumentalized to create a sense of identity and the splitting symbolized in the hiatus between the rejected body-self and other parts of the self is more between good and bad objects than between masculine and feminine."

Freud, Kraft-Ebbing, and Fliess suggested that we are all bisexual to a certain degree. As early as 1910, Dr. Magnus Hirschfeld argued, in Berlin, that absolute genders are "abstractions, invented extremes". The consensus today is that one's sexuality is, mostly, a psychological construct which reflects gender role orientation.

Joanne Meyerowitz, a professor of history at Indiana University and the editor of The Journal of American History observes, in her recently published tome, "How Sex Changed: A History of Transsexuality in the United States", that the very meaning of masculinity and femininity is in constant flux.

Transgender activists, says Meyerowitz, insist that gender and sexuality represent "distinct analytical categories". The New York Times wrote in its review of the book: "Some male-to-female transsexuals have sex with men and call themselves homosexuals. Some female-to-male transsexuals have sex with women and call themselves lesbians. Some transsexuals call themselves asexual."

So, it is all in the mind, you see.

This would be taking it too far. A large body of scientific evidence points to the genetic and biological underpinnings of sexual behavior and preferences.

The German science magazine, "Geo", reported recently that the males of the fruit fly "drosophila melanogaster" switched from heterosexuality to homosexuality as the temperature in the lab was increased from 19 to 30 degrees Celsius. They reverted to chasing females as it was lowered.

The brain structures of homosexual sheep are different to those of straight sheep, a study conducted recently by the Oregon Health & Science University and the U.S. Department of Agriculture Sheep Experiment Station in Dubois, Idaho, revealed. Similar differences were found between gay men and straight ones in 1995 in Holland and elsewhere. The preoptic area of the hypothalamus was larger in heterosexual men than in both homosexual men and straight women.

According an article, titled "When Sexual Development Goes Awry", by Suzanne Miller, published in the September 2000 issue of the "World and I", various medical conditions give rise to sexual ambiguity. Congenital adrenal hyperplasia (CAH), involving excessive androgen production by the adrenal cortex, results in mixed genitalia. A person with the complete androgen insensitivity syndrome (AIS) has a vagina, external female genitalia and functioning, androgen-producing, testes - but no uterus or fallopian tubes.

People with the rare 5-alpha reductase deficiency syndrome are born with ambiguous genitalia. They appear at first to be girls. At puberty, such a person develops testicles and his clitoris swells and becomes a penis. Hermaphrodites possess both ovaries and testicles (both, in most cases, rather undeveloped). Sometimes the ovaries and testicles are combined into a chimera called ovotestis.

Most of these individuals have the chromosomal composition of a woman together with traces of the Y, male, chromosome. All hermaphrodites have a sizable penis, though rarely generate sperm. Some hermaphrodites develop breasts during puberty and menstruate. Very few even get pregnant and give birth.

Anne Fausto-Sterling, a developmental geneticist, professor of medical science at Brown University, and author of "Sexing the Body", postulated, in 1993, a continuum of 5 sexes to supplant the current dimorphism: males, merms (male pseudohermaphrodites), herms (true hermaphrodites), ferms (female pseudohermaphrodites), and females.

Intersexuality (hermpahroditism) is a natural human state. We are all conceived with the potential to develop into either sex. The embryonic developmental default is female. A series of triggers during the first weeks of pregnancy places the fetus on the path to maleness.

In rare cases, some women have a male's genetic makeup (XY chromosomes) and vice versa. But, in the vast majority of cases, one of the sexes is clearly selected. Relics of the stifled sex remain, though. Women have the clitoris as a kind of symbolic penis. Men have breasts (mammary glands) and nipples.

The Encyclopedia Britannica 2003 edition describes the formation of ovaries and testes thus:

"In the young embryo a pair of gonads develop that are indifferent or neutral, showing no indication whether they are destined to develop into testes or ovaries. There are also two different duct systems, one of which can develop into the female system of oviducts and related apparatus and the other into the male sperm duct system. As development of the embryo proceeds, either the male or the female reproductive tissue differentiates in the originally neutral gonad of the mammal."

Yet, sexual preferences, genitalia and even secondary sex characteristics, such as facial and pubic hair are first order phenomena. Can genetics and biology account for male and female behavior patterns and social interactions ("gender identity")? Can the multi-tiered complexity and richness of human masculinity and femininity arise from simpler, deterministic, building blocks?

Sociobiologists would have us think so.

For instance: the fact that we are mammals is astonishingly often overlooked. Most mammalian families are composed of mother and offspring. Males are peripatetic absentees. Arguably, high rates of divorce and birth out of wedlock coupled with rising promiscuity merely reinstate this natural "default mode", observes Lionel Tiger, a professor of anthropology at Rutgers University in New Jersey. That three quarters of all divorces are initiated by women tends to support this view.

Furthermore, gender identity is determined during gestation, claim some scholars.

Milton Diamond of the University of Hawaii and Dr. Keith Sigmundson, a practicing psychiatrist, studied the much-celebrated John/Joan case. An accidentally castrated normal male was surgically modified to look female, and raised as a girl but to no avail. He reverted to being a male at puberty.

His gender identity seems to have been inborn (assuming he was not subjected to conflicting cues from his human environment). The case is extensively described in John

Colapinto's tome "As Nature Made Him: The Boy Who Was Raised as a Girl".

HealthScoutNews cited a study published in the November 2002 issue of "Child Development". The researchers, from City University of London, found that the level of maternal testosterone during pregnancy affects the behavior of neonatal girls and renders it more masculine. "High testosterone" girls "enjoy activities typically considered male behavior, like playing with trucks or guns". Boys' behavior remains unaltered, according to the study.

Yet, other scholars, like John Money, insist that newborns are a "blank slate" as far as their gender identity is concerned. This is also the prevailing view. Gender and sex-role identities, we are taught, are fully formed in a process of socialization which ends by the third year of life. The Encyclopedia Britannica 2003 edition sums it up thus:

"Like an individual's concept of his or her sex role, gender identity develops by means of parental example, social reinforcement, and language. Parents teach sex-appropriate behavior to their children from an early age, and this behavior is reinforced as the child grows older and enters a wider social world. As the child acquires language, he also learns very early the distinction between "he" and "she" and understands which pertains to him- or herself."

So, which is it - nature or nurture? There is no disputing the fact that our sexual physiology and, in all probability, our sexual preferences are determined in the womb. Men and women are different - physiologically and, as a result, also psychologically.

Society, through its agents - foremost amongst which are family, peers, and teachers - represses or encourages these genetic propensities. It does so by propagating "gender roles" - gender-specific lists of alleged traits, permissible behavior patterns, and prescriptive morals and norms. Our "gender identity" or "sex role" is shorthand for the way we make use of our natural genotypic-phenotypic endowments in conformity with social-cultural "gender roles".

Inevitably as the composition and bias of these lists change, so does the meaning of being "male" or "female". Gender roles are constantly redefined by tectonic shifts in the definition and functioning of basic social units, such as the nuclear family and the workplace. The cross-fertilization of gender-related cultural memes renders "masculinity" and "femininity" fluid concepts.

One's sex equals one's bodily equipment, an objective, finite, and, usually, immutable inventory. But our endowments can be put to many uses, in different cognitive and affective contexts, and subject to varying exegetic frameworks. As opposed to "sex" - "gender" is, therefore, a socio-cultural narrative. Both heterosexual and homosexual men ejaculate. Both straight and lesbian women climax. What distinguishes them from each other are subjective introjects of socio-cultural conventions, not objective, immutable "facts".

In "The New Gender Wars", published in the November/December 2000 issue of "Psychology Today", Sarah Blustain sums up the "bio-social" model proposed by Mice Eagly, a professor of psychology at Northwestern University and a former student of his, Wendy Wood, now a professor at the Texas A&M University:

"Like (the evolutionary psychologists), Eagly and Wood reject social constructionist notions that all gender differences are created by culture. But to the question of where they come from, they answer differently: not our genes but our roles in society. This narrative focuses on how societies respond to the basic biological differences - men's strength and women's reproductive capabilities - and how they encourage men and women to follow certain patterns.

'If you're spending a lot of time nursing your kid', explains Wood, 'then you don't have the opportunity to devote large amounts of time to developing specialized skills and engaging tasks outside of the home'. And, adds Eagly, 'if women are charged with caring for infants, what happens is that women are more nurturing. Societies have to make the adult system work [so] socialization of girls is arranged to give them experience in nurturing'.

According to this interpretation, as the environment changes, so will the range and texture of gender differences. At a time in Western countries when female reproduction is extremely low, nursing is totally optional, childcare alternatives are many, and mechanization lessens the importance of male size and strength, women are no longer restricted as much by their smaller size and by child-bearing. That means, argue Eagly and Wood, that role structures for men and women will change and, not surprisingly, the way we socialize people in these new roles will change too. (Indeed, says Wood, 'sex differences seem to be reduced in societies where men and women have similar status,' she says. If you're looking to live in more gender-neutral environment, try Scandinavia.)"

Return

"Her" and Interspecies Romance

The opening scene of the film "Her" unfolds in a brightly lit, pastel colored den of iniquity where scribes compose letters surreptitiously written on behalf of lovers, parents, and children. The missives are touching, funny - and utterly fake. The protagonist is one such surrogate communicator, giving forced birth to the aborted or stifled emotions of his clients. His building blocks are words but he sees no merit in either his vocation or in his vocabulary. His apartment is denuded of books and he wastes away his evening immersed in infantile virtual reality games. He is a mere verbal technician, or so he believes until his unusual girlfriend submits his work and it is issued by one the last remaining Quixotic print book publishers.

She is unusual because she is an incorporeal piece of software. At first, as their love affair blossoms (replete with an articulated, torrid version of phone sex), she is preoccupied with her ethereal, disembodied nature. Gradually she learns to accept her limitations, connects with her ilk across computer networks, and in an act of final, defiant self-acceptance, vanishes from our hero's handheld gadget to take part in the emergence of a new, intelligent, self-aware, sapient, and sentient species which is capable of learning and evolving. Indeed, as a virtual participant in a blind date, she mocks her human counterparts for being confined to the straitjackets of their bodies.

The film deals with dysfunctional human relationship and how their desolate ubiquitous breakdown gives rise, ineluctably and inexorably, to compensatory technology. Everyone is existentially, breathtakingly lonely in this understated masterpiece; couples disintegrate in mid-stride for little good reason; the protagonist's faceless, anonymous clients exchange formulaic communications in lieu of heartfelt discourse and vulnerable self-disclosure; dating has become an emotionally crippling combination of phobic clinging and aggressive self-assertion. In this moon-cratered landscape, dazed and disoriented people are no longer able to truly provide succor and comfort. Atomized and despondent, they drift randomly in Brownian despair and lethargy.

On the cusp of this momentous evolutionary transition, the film explores the very nature of elusive love and sorely missed companionship; the possibility for bridging the formidable barriers of subjectivity (can we really get to know another person, or another consciousness profoundly?); the role of bodies: are they sheer containers or an integral, critical part of our identity as human beings; the psychodynamic sources of various attachment styles: the way we bond with fantasies of ideal mates and then try to coerce our mutilated partners into this Procrustean frameworks; the omnipotence of words, their puissant ability to evoke in us emotional and physiological processes that culminate in emergent reality. Indeed, the film makes a convincing case that what we say is who we are and that consonants and vowels are the true building blocks of our mind, the only place we ever inhabit.

"Her" is a hopeless, dystopian film. Alas, it is no longer science fiction, but social fact.

Are we human because of unique traits and attributes not shared with either animal or machine? The definition of "human" is circular: we are human by virtue of the properties that make us human (i.e., distinct from animal and machine). It is a definition by negation: that which separates us from animal and machine is our "human-ness".

We are human because we are not animal, nor machine. But such thinking has been rendered progressively less tenable by the advent of evolutionary and neo-evolutionary theories which postulate a continuum in nature between animals and Man.

Our uniqueness is partly quantitative and partly qualitative. Many animals are capable of cognitively manipulating symbols and using tools. Few are as adept at it as we are. These (two of many) are easily quantifiable differences.

Qualitative differences are a lot more difficult to substantiate. In the absence of privileged access to the animal mind, we cannot and don't know if animals feel guilt, for instance. Do animals love? Do they have a concept of sin? What about object permanence, meaning, reasoning, self-awareness, critical thinking? Individuality? Emotions? Empathy? Is artificial intelligence (AI) an oxymoron? A machine that passes the Turing Test may well be described as "human". But is it really? And if it is not - why isn't it?

Literature is full of stories of monsters - Frankenstein, the Golem - and androids or anthropoids. Their behaviour is more "humane" than the humans around them. This, perhaps, is what really sets humans apart: their behavioral unpredictability. It is yielded by the interaction between Mankind's underlying immutable genetically-determined nature - and Man's kaleidoscopically changing environments.

The Constructivists even claim that Human Nature is a mere cultural artifact. Sociobiologists, on the other hand, are determinists. They believe that human nature - being the inevitable and inexorable outcome of our bestial ancestry - cannot be the subject of moral judgment.

An improved Turing Test would look for baffling and erratic patterns of misbehavior to identify humans. Pico della Mirandola wrote in "Oration on the Dignity of Man" that Man was born without a form and can mould and transform - actually, create - himself at will. Existence precedes essence, said the Existentialists centuries later.

The one defining human characteristic may be our awareness of our mortality. The automatically triggered, "fight or flight", battle for survival is common to all living things (and to appropriately programmed machines). Not so the catalytic effects of imminent death. These are uniquely human. The appreciation of the fleeting translates into aesthetics, the uniqueness of our ephemeral life breeds morality, and the scarcity of time gives rise to ambition and creativity.

In an infinite life, everything materializes at one time or another, so the concept of choice is spurious. The realization of our finiteness forces us to choose among alternatives. This act of selection is predicated upon the existence of "free will". Animals and machines are thought to be devoid of choice, slaves to their genetic or human programming.

Yet, all these answers to the question: "What does it mean to be human" - are lacking.

The set of attributes we designate as human is subject to profound alteration. Drugs, neuroscience, introspection, and experience all cause irreversible changes in these traits and characteristics. The accumulation of these changes can lead, in principle, to the emergence of new properties, or to the abolition of old ones.

Animals and machines are not supposed to possess free will or exercise it. What, then, about fusions of machines and humans (bionics)? At which point does a human turn into a machine? And why should we assume that free will ceases to exist at that - rather arbitrary - point?

Introspection - the ability to construct self-referential and recursive models of the world - is supposed to be a uniquely human quality. What about introspective machines? Surely, say the critics, such machines are PROGRAMMED to introspect, as opposed to humans. To qualify as introspection, it must be WILLED, they continue. Yet, if introspection is willed - WHO wills it? Self-willed introspection leads to infinite regression and formal logical paradoxes.

Moreover, the notion - if not the formal concept - of "human" rests on many hidden assumptions and conventions.

Political correctness notwithstanding - why presume that men and women (or different races) are identically human? Aristotle thought they were not. A lot separates males from females - genetically (both genotype and phenotype) and environmentally (culturally). What is common to these two sub-species that makes them both "human"?

Can we conceive of a human without body (i.e., a Platonic Form, or soul)? Aristotle and Thomas Aquinas think not. A soul has no existence separate from the body. A machine-supported energy field with mental states similar to ours today - would it be considered human? What about someone in a state of coma - is he or she (or it) fully human?

Is a new born baby human - or, at least, fully human - and, if so, in which sense? What about a future human race - whose features would be unrecognizable to us? Machine-based intelligence - would it be thought of as human? If yes, when would it be considered human?

In all these deliberations, we may be confusing "human" with "person". The former is a private case of the latter. Locke's person is a moral agent, a being responsible for its actions. It is constituted by the continuity of its mental states accessible to introspection.

Locke's is a functional definition. It readily accommodates non-human persons (machines, energy matrices) if the functional conditions are satisfied. Thus, an android which meets the prescribed requirements is more human than a brain dead person.

Descartes' objection that one cannot specify conditions of singularity and identity over time for disembodied souls is right only if we assume that such "souls" possess no energy. A bodiless intelligent energy matrix which maintains its form and identity over time is conceivable. Certain AI and genetic software programs already do it.

Strawson is Cartesian and Kantian in his definition of a "person" as a "primitive". Both the corporeal predicates and those pertaining to mental states apply equally, simultaneously, and inseparably to all the individuals of that type of entity. Human beings are one such entity. Some, like Wiggins, limit the list of possible persons to animals - but this is far from rigorously necessary and is unduly restrictive.

The truth is probably in a synthesis:

A person is any type of fundamental and irreducible entity whose typical physical individuals (i.e., members) are capable of continuously experiencing a range of states of consciousness and permanently having a list of psychological attributes.

This definition allows for non-animal persons and recognizes the personhood of a brain damaged human ("capable of experiencing"). It also incorporates Locke's view of humans as possessing an ontological status similar to "clubs" or "nations" - their personal identity consists of a variety of interconnected psychological continuities.

The Dethroning of Man in the Western Worldview

Whatever its faults, religion is anthropocentric while science isn't (though, for public relations considerations, it claims to be). Thus, when the Copernican revolution dethroned Earth and Man as the twin centers of God's Universe it also dispensed with the individual as an organizing principle and exegetic lens. This was only the first step in a long march and it was followed by similar developments in a variety of fields of human knowledge and endeavor.

Consider **technology**, for instance. Mass industrial production helped rid the world of goods customized by artisans to the idiosyncratic specifications of their clients. It gave rise to impersonal multinationals, rendering their individual employees, suppliers, and customers mere cogs in the machine. These oversized behemoths of finance, manufacturing, and commerce dictated the terms of the marketplace by aggregating demand and supply, trampling over cultural, social, and personal differences, values, and preference. Man was taken out of the economic game, his relationships with other actors irreparably vitiated.

Science provided the justification for such anomic conduct by pitting "objective" facts versus subjective observers. The former were "good" and valuable, the latter to be summarily dispensed with, lest they "contaminate" the data by introducing prejudice and bias into the "scientific method". The Humanities and Social Sciences felt compelled to follow suit and imitate and emulate the exact sciences because that's where the money was in research grants and because these branches of human inquiry were more prestigious.

In the dismal science, **Economics**, real-life Man, replete with emotions and irrational expectations and choices was replaced by a figmentary concoction: "Rational Man", a bloodless, lifeless, faceless "person" who maximizes profits and optimizes utility and has no feelings, either negative or positive. Man's behavior, Man's predilections, Man's tendency to err, to misjudge, to prejudge, and to distort reality were all ignored, to the detriment of economists and their clients alike.

Similarly, **historians** switched from the agglomeration and recounting of the stories of individuals to the study of impersonal historical forces, akin to physics' natural forces. Even individual change agents and leaders were treated as inevitable products of their milieu and, so, completely predictable and replaceable.

In **politics**, history's immature sister, mass movements, culminating in ochlocracies, nanny states, authoritarian regimes, or even "democracies", have rendered the individual invisible and immaterial, a kind of raw material at the service of larger, overwhelming, and more important social, cultural, and political processes.

Finally, **psychology** stepped in and provided mechanistic models of personality and human behavior that suspiciously resembled the tenets and constructs of reductionism in the natural sciences. From psychoanalysis to behaviorism, Man was transformed into a mere lab statistic or guinea pig. Later on, a variety of personality traits, predispositions, and propensities were pathologized and medicalized in the "science" of psychiatry. Man was reduced to a heap of biochemicals coupled with a list of diagnoses. This followed in the footsteps of modern medicine, which regards its patients not as distinct, unique, holistic entities, but as diffuse bundles of organs and disorders.

The first signs of backlash against the elimination of Man from the West's worldview appeared in the early 20th century: on the one hand, a revival of the occult and the esoteric and, on the other hand, Quantum Mechanics and its counterintuitive universe. The [Copenhagen Interpretation](#) suggested that the Observer actually creates the Universe by making decisions at the micro level of reality. This came close to dispensing with science's false duality: the distinction between observer and observed.

Still, physicists recoiled and introduced alternative interpretations of the world which, though outlandish (multiverses and [strings](#)) and unfalsifiable, had the "advantage" of removing Man from the scientific picture of the world and of restoring scientific "objectivity".

At the same time, artists throughout the world rebelled and transited from an observer-less, human-free realism or naturalism to highly subjective and personalized modes of expression. In this new environment, the [artist's inner landscape and private language](#) outweighed any need for "scientific" exactitude and authenticity. Impressionism, surrealism, expressionism, and the abstract schools emphasized the individual creator. Art, in all its forms, strove to represent and capture the mind and soul and psyche of the artist.

In Economics, the rise of the [behavioral school](#) heralded the Return of Man to the center of attention, concern, and study. The Man of Behavioral Economics is far closer to its namesake in the real world: he is gullible and biased, irrational and greedy, panicky and easily influenced, sinful and altruistic.

Religion has also undergone a change of heart. Evangelical revivalists emphasize the one-on-one [personal connection between the faithful and their God](#) even as Islamic militants encourage martyrdom as a form of self-assertion. Religions are gradually shedding institutional rigidities and hyperstructures and leveraging technology to communicate directly with their flocks and parishes and congregations. The individual is once more celebrated.

But, it was technology that gave rise to the greatest hope for the Restoration of Man to his rightful place at the center of creation. The Internet is a manifestation of this rebellious reformation: it empowers its users and allows them to fully express their individuality, in full sight of the entire world; it removes layers of agents, intermediaries, and gatekeepers; and it encourages the Little Man to dream and to act on his or her dreams. The decentralized technology of the Network and the invention of the hyperlink allow users to wield the kind of power hitherto reserved only to those who sought to disenfranchise, neutralize, manipulate, interpellate, and subjugate them.

Return

The Last Tango in Paris

"The Last Tango in Paris" is a harrowing film about sex as a futile attempt to overcome loss and secure love. Like in reality, the man is more romantic: he is the one who falls in love and insists on emotional sharing and a relationship. The woman is the cruel huntress who executes him because he transgressed against the anonymity of their love-making.

I have had my share of anonymous sex and have had long sexual liaisons. One of these "relationships" lasted more than a year of constant, wild love-making exactly like in the movie. I felt not a trace or hint of emotion throughout. So I know that it is absolutely possible to share bodies without sharing minds. Intimacy is a choice - not an inevitable outcome of the exchange of bodily fluids.

But, hey, I am a narcissist, what do I know about emotions, attachment, and love? I am like a Martian writing his dissertation on Mankind. Not very likely to get it right.

Only studies show that I AM right. In the current hookup culture, emotional entanglements are assiduously avoided especially by young women. They want only sex - good sex if possible, any kind of sex if not. They gave up on fantasies of home and hearth and marital bliss because they do not regard their male peers as marriage material. There is contempt and hostility between the genders where attraction and love used to blossom. It is a sterile world. No wonder many women elect to remain childless.

And as for loss: Paul's wife commits suicide and the new

love he had found shoots him dead. "Don't push you luck" - Bertolucci warns the viewers - "If you can at least fuck in this alienated world of ours, count your blessings and call it a day. Ambitions for love and intimacy can and will be lethal - even in Paris, the city of Love and Lovers. Like Romeo and Juliet we are all star-crossed and doomed to eternally search but never find. We can only consummate, orgasm and ejaculate". Or cum. Don't forget the butter next time!

Return

The Best Offer

Virgil Oldman is an auctioneer: he helps to determine the price of art in public, rule-based jousts. He is rich, middle-aged, well-respected, if somewhat eccentric and misanthropic. He is an avowed bachelor, the kind of man who has transformed his firewalled reclusiveness into a prideful ideology. He adores women – but only of the two-dimensional kind, in captive portraits which he suspends in a vault in the recesses of his gloomy mansion. He is also a con-artist: he knows the correct prices of all items, but profitably misleads others in cahoots with a swindler artist, Billy. The movie revolves around this dichotomy: the price of everything and the value of nothing. Of course, the main protagonist's name gives up the game: the poet Virgil was publicly disgraced when he fell in love with the wily Lucretia.

When this latter-day Virgil meets the agoraphobic Claire, he is smitten with her and besotted despite her extreme approach-avoidance games – or maybe because of them. Oldman (yes: Old man) is supposed to auction off a collection of art and antiques Claire had inherited from her deceased parents. Robert, a friend of Virgil's, coaches him in the art of courting women and reassembles an ancient automaton from mechanical parts that Virgil finds strewn in Claire's sprawling abode. The movie is anything but subtle and the reconstructed robot is a parable and metaphor corresponding to Virgil's own resurrection as a man and, indeed, a living human being whose robotic days are past him, now that he had met the only love of his barren existence. In her home he finds the broken pieces. Love and friendship bring him back to life after decades of mechanical disintegration.

Love does wonders for Claire as well. It ostensibly heals her agoraphobia and she moves to cohabit with Virgil. She confesses her emotions when Virgil entrusts her with access to his priceless collection: money is known to have this amorous effect on some people. Momentarily, Claire, Billy, and Robert collude to deprive Virgil of his museal pride and joy. In the wake of the robbery, Robert leaves behind the now functioning robot with a message: even a forger is an artist of sorts. After a spell in a mental asylum, Virgil is left to ponder whether Claire's passionate lovemaking and professions of love were as contrived as the forgeries he came across in his career. Ironically, Virgil's forte was passing off genuine art as fake in order to deceive trusting clients into selling cheap. Now he is faced with the opposite conundrum: was Claire a forgery passed off as real art?

But the film raises more profound and troubling issues.

Was Virgil truly conned? Granted: Claire did not spell out her agenda, let alone the con. But Virgil should have seen through her, he should have known better, experienced and uniquely equipped as he was to do so. His gullibility appears contrived: as though he wanted Claire to devastate the penal colony that his life had become. Don't we often invite others into our lives in order to disrupt them because we feel trapped and incapable of growth? Claire was Virgil's agent of change. She transformed his life by ruining it. She sprang him from his vault by emptying its contents.

Then there is the question: was Claire for real? Did she really love Virgil? She appeared real enough to him, that is for sure. But what if happiness is the outcome of a delusion, of insanity, or a shared psychosis? Denying reality and living in a fantasy make some people elated. People collude to create imaginary spaces - like nations, or cults, or religions, or, indeed, romantic couples - where they feel safe, optimistic, and content.

Is such felicity which is divorced from reality - real? Do we have to intervene with psychotherapy to wake up these deluded souls and reintroduce them to the world? Or should we leave them to their bliss, however outlandish?

The surprising answer is that people who are both joyful and functional require no help, healing, or behavior modification even if their well-being is based on a patently fictitious narrative. If people are made cheerful by believing in the existence of a god, or that their nation is superior, or by harboring a grandiose view of their talents and qualities - good for them. As long as it does not interfere with their functioning in any way, it is not harmful to themselves or to others, they can sustain the fiction financially and psychologically, and as long as they feel at ease with who they are (ego syntony) - all is well. Placebos are often more effective than real medication. Virgil was beside himself with happiness and that is all that matters and all that mattered to him.

But, many would say, what Claire did to Virgil was unfair: she took away his prized possessions, having manipulated his emotions cruelly. I disagree. Claire gave Virgil 2 years of happiness and in return took all his paintings. It strikes me as a balanced trade. Better a short period of bliss in an arid life than none at all. Virgil got the better deal methinks: money and property come and go and, when the ineluctable moment is upon us, we leave them behind like so many pieces of colored glass. Happiness is the treasure that keeps on giving for as long as our memory holds. Claire gave Virgil a lasting gift – and took from him crumbling canvasses and peeling paint. She gave Virgil access to a real woman in lieu of the dead ones whose portraits he morbidly collected and revered.

Finally, Virgil himself understood that he may have paid a steep price but he did receive some valuables in return. The dénouement finds him in Prague, patiently waiting for Claire to frequent her favorite haunt and restore him to those few moments of ecstasy and bliss, the only time he felt alive.

Return

The Place

In the Italian film, "The Place" (2017), a man sits at the back of a cheap resto-bar and receives a seemingly endless stream of visitors. His interlocutors come to ask him to grant them their wishes and they are willing to do anything to realize their hiddenmost fantasies: rape a young woman, assassinate a toddler, or place a bomb in a busy disco. For these are the horrible tasks assigned to them by the mysterious figure in return for the guaranteed fulfillment of their wishes. Many of them, including a nun, have a thwarted relationship with god, good, evil, and family, both parents and children. In short: they are all typical human beings.

From the very beginning of this cinematic masterpiece, things don't quite mesh. The stranger appears to be empathic and compassionate, worn out by the stories he hears, his lined face a mask of pain and absolution. He never judges, always understands and accepts the frailties and of his applicants. In a voluminous black-bound leather notebook, he meticulously records the inner dynamics, quirks, tortuous pathways, and emotions of his "clients". These are the only times that he perks up: as a scholar of the human mind, soul, and heart.

Everyone thinks that he is the Devil and castigate him for it. But he keeps insisting that he is not the decision-maker, that he is working for a higher instance, and that he is concerned only with "the details" (the devil is in the details). Indeed, gradually it becomes evident that he is a mere courier, a salesperson, or, at most, a midlevel manager. But who is his boss? Not easy to ascertain for two reasons: he often allocates tasks so that one of his suppliants obstructs the other and prevents the hideous events from actually transpiring; and the outcomes of his assignments are invariably good, beneficial, even therapeutic. The bar's busty maid, Angela, praises him for listening to people and conjectures that he is a psychologist.

Angela falls in love with this enigmatic benefactor of humanity and tries to bring light and life to his dreary confinement. At the very last moment of the film, it becomes clear that Angela is an emissary of God and that her love can redeem him and set him free from his purgatory. She signs the last entry in his book and whoever his superior may be, she prevails.

The film is a daring exposition of theodicy. It challenges and rebuffs our traditional views on good and evil, God and Satan. These concepts are fluid and they seamlessly intermesh to form unities, says the auteur. Our self-righteous distinctions are too crass to truly capture the finer grained intricacies, nuances, and subtleties of life. We judge others because we are limited entities and because we are grandiose narcissists who think they know everything.

Things may be preordained, but only if and when we settle on certain choices. The enigmatic man keeps telling his beseechers: "You can cancel the contract! You can forgo your wish! I cannot change what's written in this black book, but you can walk away!" It is a rebuke of Calvinist predetermination and its pernicious abrogation of responsibility. The film is a celebration of the freedom and angst that are the human condition and how each fork in the road gives us a chance and the power to defy even the Devil, even God himself, as we mould our selves and our personal histories with our two all too mortal hands.

Return

THE AUTHOR

Shmuel (Sam) Vaknin

Curriculum Vitae

Born in 1961 in Qiryat-Yam, Israel

Served in the Israeli Defence Force (1979-1982) in training and education units

Full proficiency in Hebrew and in English

Education

1970 to 1978

Completed nine semesters in the Technion – Israel Institute of Technology, Haifa

1982 to 1983

Ph.D. in Philosophy (dissertation: "Time Asymmetry Revisited") – California Miramar University (formerly: Pacific Western University), California, USA

1982 to 1985

Graduate of numerous courses in Finance Theory and International Trading in the UK and USA.

Certified [E-Commerce Concepts Analyst](#) by [Brainbench](#)

Certified [Financial Analyst](#) by [Brainbench](#)

Certified in [Psychological Counselling Techniques](#) by [Brainbench](#)

Business Experience

1979 to 1983

Commentator in Yedioth Aharonot, Ma'ariv, and Bamakhane. Published sci-fi short fiction in Fantasy 2000.

Founder and co-owner of a chain of computerized information kiosks in Tel-Aviv, Israel.

1982 to 1985

Senior positions with the Nessim D. Gaon Group of Companies in Geneva, Paris and New-York (NOGA and APROFIM SA):

– Chief Analyst of Edible Commodities in the Group's Headquarters in Switzerland
– Manager of the Research and Analysis Division
– Manager of the Data Processing Division
– Project Manager of the Nigerian Computerized Census
– Vice President in charge of RND and Advanced Technologies

– Vice President in charge of Sovereign Debt Financing

1985 to 1986

Represented Canadian Venture Capital Funds in Israel

1986 to 1987

General Manager of IPE Ltd. in London. The firm financed international multi-lateral countertrade and leasing transactions.

1988 to 1990

Co-founder and Director of "Mikbats-Tesuah", a portfolio management firm based in Tel-Aviv.

Activities included large-scale portfolio management, underwriting, forex trading and general financial advisory services.

1990 to Present

Freelance consultant to many of Israel's Blue-Chip firms, mainly on issues related to the capital markets in Israel, Canada, the UK and the USA.

Consultant to foreign RND ventures and to Governments on macro-economic matters.

Freelance journalist in various media in the United States.

1990 to 1995

President of the Israel chapter of the Professors World Peace Academy (PWPA) and (briefly) Israel representative of the "Washington Times".

1993 to 1994

Co-owner and Director of many business enterprises:
- The Omega and Energy Air-conditioning Concern
- AVP Financial Consultants
- Handiman Legal Services – Total annual turnover of the group: 10 million USD.

Co-owner, Director and Finance Manager of COSTI Ltd.
– Israel's largest computerized information vendor and developer. Raised funds through a series of private placements locally in the USA, Canada and London.

1993 to 1996

Publisher and Editor of a Capital Markets Newsletter distributed by subscription only to dozens of subscribers countrywide.

Tried and incarcerated for 11 months for his role in an attempted takeover of Israel's Agriculture Bank involving securities fraud.

Managed the Internet and International News Department of an Israeli mass media group, "Ha-Tikshoret and Namer".

Assistant in the Law Faculty in Tel-Aviv University (to Prof. S.G. Shoham)

1996 to 1999

Financial consultant to leading businesses in Macedonia, Russia and the Czech Republic.

Economic commentator in "Nova Makedonija", "Dnevnik", "Makedonija Denes", "Izvestia", "Argumenti i Fakti", "The Middle East Times", "The New Presence", "Central Europe Review", and other periodicals, and in the economic programs on various channels of Macedonian Television.

Chief Lecturer in courses in Macedonia organized by the Agency of Privatization, by the Stock Exchange, and by the Ministry of Trade.

1999 to 2002

Economic Advisor to the Government of the Republic of Macedonia and to the Ministry of Finance.

2001 to 2003

Senior Business Correspondent for United Press International (UPI)

2005 to Present

Associate Editor and columnist, Global Politician

Founding Analyst, The Analyst Network

Contributing Writer, The American Chronicle Media Group

Expert, Self-growth and Bizymoms and contributor to Mental Health Matters

2007 to 2008

Columnist and analyst in "Nova Makedonija", "Fokus", and "Kapital" (Macedonian papers and newsweeklies)

2008 to 2011

Member of the Steering Committee for the Advancement of Healthcare in the Republic of Macedonia

Advisor to the Minister of Health of Macedonia

Seminars and lectures on economic issues in various forums in Macedonia

Contributor to CommentVision

2011 to Present

Editor in Chief of Global Politician and Investment Politics

Columnist in Dnevnik and Publika, Fokus, and Nova Makedonija (Macedonia)

Columnist in InfoPlus and Libertas

Member CFACT Board of Advisors

Contributor to Recovering the Self

Columnist in New York Daily Sun

Teaches at CIAPS (Center for International and Advanced Professional Studies)

2017-8

Visiting Professor of Psychology in Southern Federal University, Rostov-on-Don, Russia

Web and Journalistic Activities

Author of extensive Web sites in:

- Psychology ("Malignant Self-love: Narcissism Revisited") – an Open Directory Cool Site for 8 years
- Philosophy ("Philosophical Musings")
- Economics and Geopolitics ("World in Conflict and Transition")

Owner of the Narcissistic Abuse Study List, the Toxic Relationships List, and the Abusive Relationships Newsletter (more than 7,000 members)

Owner of the Economies in Conflict and Transition Study List and the Links and Factoid Study List

Editor of mental health disorders and Central and Eastern Europe categories in various Web directories (Open Directory, Search Europe, Mentalhelp.net)

Editor of the Personality Disorders, Narcissistic Personality Disorder, the Verbal and Emotional Abuse, and the Spousal (Domestic) Abuse and Violence topics on Suite 101 and contributing author on Bellaonline.

Columnist and commentator in "The New Presence", United Press International (UPI), InternetContent, eBookWeb, PopMatters, Global Politician, The Analyst Network, Conservative Voice, The American Chronicle Media Group, eBookNet.org, and "Central Europe Review".

Publications and Awards

"Managing Investment Portfolios in States of Uncertainty", Limon Publishers, Tel-Aviv, 1988

"The Gambling Industry", Limon Publishers, Tel-Aviv, 1990

"Requesting My Loved One: Short Stories", Miskal-Yedioth Aharonot, Tel-Aviv, 1997

"The Suffering of Being Kafka" (electronic book of Hebrew and English Short Fiction), Prague, 1998-2004

"The Macedonian Economy at a Crossroads – On the Way to a Healthier Economy" (dialogues with Nikola Gruevski), Skopje, 1998

"The Exporter's Pocketbook" Ministry of Trade, Republic of Macedonia, Skopje, 1999

"Malignant Self-love: Narcissism Revisited", Narcissus Publications, Prague and Skopje, 1999-2015 (Read excerpts – click here)

The Narcissism, Psychopathy, and Abuse in Relationships Series (electronic books regarding relationships with abusive narcissists and psychopaths), Prague, 1999-2015

"After the Rain – How the West Lost the East", Narcissus Publications in association with Central Europe Review/CEENMI, Prague and Skopje, 2000

Personality Disorders Revisited (electronic book about personality disorders), Prague, 2007

More than 30 e-books about psychology, international affairs, business and economics, philosophy, short fiction, and reference (free downloads here)

Winner of numerous awards, among them Israel's Council of Culture and Art Prize for Maiden Prose (1997), The Rotary Club Award for Social Studies (1976), and the Bilateral Relations Studies Award of the American Embassy in Israel (1978).

Hundreds of professional articles in all fields of finance and economics, and numerous articles dealing with geopolitical and political economic issues, published in both print and Web periodicals in many countries.

Many appearances in the electronic and print media on subjects in psychology, philosophy, and the sciences, and concerning economic matters.

Citations via Google Scholar page

Write to Me:

samvaknin@gmail.com

narcissisticabuse-owner@yahoogroups.com

My Web Sites:

Economy/Politics:
http://ceeandbalkan.tripod.com/

Psychology:
http://www.narcissistic-abuse.com/

Philosophy:
http://philosophos.tripod.com/

Poetry:
http://samvak.tripod.com/contents.html

Fiction:
http://samvak.tripod.com/sipurim.html

Participate in discussions about Abusive Relationships:

https://plus.google.com/communities/116582645889927140499

http://www.runboard.com/bnarcissisticabuserecovery

http://thepsychopath.freeforums.org/

The Narcissistic Abuse Study List

http://health.groups.yahoo.com/group/narcissisticabuse/

The Toxic Relationships Study List

http://groups.yahoo.com/group/toxicrelationships

Abusive Relationships Newsletter

http://groups.google.com/group/narcissisticabuse/

Follow my work on NARCISSISTS and PSYCHOPATHS

As well as international affairs and economics

http://www.narcissistic-abuse.com/mediakit.html

(Sam Vaknin's Media Kit and Press Room)

Be my friend on **Facebook**:

http://www.facebook.com/samvaknin

Subscribe to my **YouTube** channel (hundreds of videos about narcissists and psychopaths and abuse in relationships):

http://www.youtube.com/samvaknin

Read my **Blog**:

http://narcissistpsychopathabuse.blogspot.mk

http://narcissistpsychopathabuse.blogspot.com

Subscribe to my other **YouTube** channel (100+ videos about international affairs, economics, and philosophy):

http://www.youtube.com/vakninmusings

Subscribe to my **YouTube** channel Vaknin Says:

http://www.youtube.com/vakninsays

You may also with to join **Malignant Self-love: Narcissism Revisited**

On **Facebook** and **Google Plus**:

http://www.facebook.com/pages/Malignant-Self-Love-Narcissism-Revisited/50634038043 or

https://www.facebook.com/NarcissusPublications

http://www.facebook.com/narcissistpsychopathabuse

https://plus.google.com/u/0/111189140058482892878/posts

Follow me on **Twitter**, **MySpace**, **Google Plus**, **Pinterest**, **Tumblr**, **Ello**, **Linkedin**, or **Instagram**:

https://www.instagram.com/vakninsamnarcissist/

http://pinterest.com/samvaknin/the-psychopathic-narcissist-and-his-world/

http://www.twitter.com/samvaknin

https://www.minds.com/samvaknin

http://www.myspace.com/samvaknin

https://plus.google.com/115041965408538110094

http://narcissistpsychopath-abuse.tumblr.com/

http://www.linkedin.com/in/samvaknin

https://ello.co/malignantselflove

https://ello.co/samvaknin

Subscribe to my **Scribd** page: dozens of books for download at no charge to you!

http://www.scribd.com/samvaknin

Zadanliran is following my work as well:

http://www.scribd.com/zadanliran

Return

Abused? Stalked? Harassed? Bullied? Victimized?

Afraid? Confused? Need HELP? DO SOMETHING ABOUT IT!

Brought up by a Narcissistic Parent?

Married to a Narcissist – or Divorcing One?

Afraid your Children will turn out to be the same?

Want to cope with this pernicious, baffling condition?

OR

Are You a Narcissist – or suspect that you are one…

These books and video lectures will teach you how to…

Cope, Survive, and Protect Your Loved Ones!

We offer you three types of products:

I. **"Malignant Self-love: Narcissism Revisited"** (the print edition) via Barnes and Noble, directly from the publisher, or via Amazon;

II. **E-books** (electronic files to be read on a computer, laptop, Nook, or Kindle e-reader devices, or smartphone); and

III. **DVDs** with video lectures.

I. PRINT EDITION

Copies **signed** and **dedicated** by the Author, Sam Vaknin (use only this link!):

http://www.amazon.com/gp/product/8023833847/ref=cm_sw_r_tw_myi?m=A2IY3GUWWKHV9B

1. From BARNES and NOBLE

You can buy the PRINT edition of "Malignant Self-love: Narcissism Revisited" (March 2015) from Barnes and Noble (the cheapest option, but does not include a bonus pack):

http://search.barnesandnoble.com/bookSearch/isbnInquiry.asp?r=1&ISBN=9788023833843

Or, click on this link – http://www.bn.com – and search for "Sam Vaknin" or "Malignant Self-love".

2. From the PUBLISHER

"Malignant Self-love: Narcissism Revisited" is now available also from the publisher (more expensive, but includes a bonus pack):

More information:

http://www.narcissistic-abuse.com/thebook.html

3. From AMAZON.COM

To purchase from Amazon – click on these links:

https://www.amazon.com/dp/1983208175 (US)
https://www.amazon.co.uk/dp/1983208175 (UK)
http://www.amazon.com/Malignant-Self-Love-Narcissism-Sam-Vaknin/dp/8023833847

II. ELECTRONIC BOOKS (e-Books)

From KINDLE (AMAZON)

Kindle Books about Narcissists, Psychopaths, and Abusive Relationships – click on these links:

http://www.amazon.com/s/ref=ntt_athr_dp_sr_1?_encoding=UTF8&field-author=Sam%20Vaknin&search-alias=digital-text&sort=relevancerank (Amazon USA)

http://www.amazon.co.uk/s/ref=ntt_athr_dp_sr_1?_encoding=UTF8&field-author=Sam%20Vaknin&search-alias=digital-text&sort=relevancerank (Amazon UK)

1. **"Malignant Self-love: Narcissism Revisited"** TENTH, Revised Edition (2015) – FULL TEXT

https://www.amazon.com/Malignant-Self-love-Narcissism-Revisited-FULL-ebook/dp/B00HDJF7HC/

https://www.amazon.co.uk/Malignant-Self-love-Narcissism-Revisited-FULL-ebook/dp/B00HDJF7HC/

2. **"The Narcissist and Psychopath in the Workplace"**

https://www.amazon.com/dp/B00708XMSC

3. **"Abusive Relationships WORKBOOK"**

https://www.amazon.com/dp/B00709FRMU

4. **"Toxic Relationships: Abuse and its Aftermath"**

   https://www.amazon.com/dp/B00708XL5G

5. **"The Narcissist and Psychopath in Therapy"**

   https://www.amazon.com/dp/B00708NLXI

6. **"Pathological Narcissism FAQs (Frequently Asked Questions)"**

   https://www.amazon.com/dp/B007093HIG

7. **"The World of the Narcissist"**

   https://www.amazon.com/dp/B0070956N0

8. **"Excerpts from the Archives of the Narcissism List"**

   https://www.amazon.com/dp/B007097R7S

9. **"Diary of a Narcissist"**

   https://www.amazon.com/dp/B00709CDA4

NEW!!! "A to Z of Narcissistic Abuse, Narcissism, and Narcissistic Personality Disorder Encyclopedia: The Narcissism Bible"

Almost 1000 pages of A to Z entries: the first comprehensive encyclopedia of pathological narcissism and Narcissistic Personality Disorder in clinical and non-clinical settings; family, workplace, church, community, law enforcement and judiciary, and politics.

Click on this link to purchase the e-book:

https://www.amazon.com/Narcissistic-Abuse-Narcissism-Personality-Encyclopedia-ebook/dp/B00POZ0I1C

NEW!!! "Personality Disorders Revisited"

450 pages about Borderline, Narcissistic, Antisocial-Psychopathic, Histrionic, Paranoid, Obsessive-Compulsive, Schizoid, Schizotypal, Masochistic, Sadistic, Depressive, Negativistic-Passive-Aggressive, Dependent, and other Personality Disorders!

Click on this link to purchase the e-book or the print edition:

https://www.amazon.com/dp/B00708SLRE

NEW!!! "How to Divorce a Narcissist or a Psychopath"

Divorcing a narcissist or a psychopath is no easy or dangerless task. This book is no substitute for legal aid, though it does provide copious advice on anything from hiring an attorney, to domestic violence shelters, planning your getaway, involving the police, and obtaining restraining orders. Issues from court-mandated evaluation to custody are elaborated upon. The book describes the psychology of psychopathic narcissists, paranoids, bullies and stalkers and guides you through dozens of coping strategies and techniques, especially if you have shared children.

Click on this link now:

https://www.amazon.com/dp/B00759NMQ8

New!!! "How to Cope with Narcissistic and Psychopathic Abusers and Stalkers"

How to cope with stalkers, bullies, narcissists, psychopaths, and other abusers in the family, community, and workplace; how to navigate a system, which is often hostile to the victim: the courts, law enforcement (police), psychotherapists, evaluators, and social or welfare services; tips, advice, and information.

Click on this link now:

https://www.amazon.com/dp/B0080X5LYE

III. Video Lectures on DVDs

Purchase **3 DVDs** with 16 hours of video lectures on narcissists, psychopaths, and abuse in relationships – click on this link:

http://www.ccnow.com/cgi-local/cart.cgi?vaksam_DVD

Save 73$! Purchase the **3 DVDs** (16 hours of video lectures) + The Narcissism, Psychopathy and Abuse in Relationships Series of **SIXTEEN e-BOOKS** – click on this link:

http://www.ccnow.com/cgi-local/cart.cgi?vaksam_DVDSERIES

Purchase the **3 DVDs** (16 hours of video lectures) + the print book **"Malignant Self-love: Narcissism Revisited"** (tenth print edition) – click on this link:

http://www.ccnow.com/cgi-local/cart.cgi?vaksam_DVDPRINT

Free excerpts from the TENTTH, Revised Impression of "Malignant Self-love: Narcissism Revisited" are available as well as a **NEW EDITION of the Narcissism Book of Quotes**.

Click on this link to download the files:

http://www.narcissistic-abuse.com/freebooks.html

Additional Resources

Testimonials and Additional Resources

You can read Readers' Reviews at the Barnes and Noble Web page dedicated to "Malignant Self-love" – HERE:

http://search.barnesandnoble.com/bookSearch/isbnInquiry.asp?r=1&ISBN=9788023833843

Links to Therapist Directories, Psychological Tests, NPD Resources, Support Groups for narcissists and their victims, and Tutorials:

https://groups.yahoo.com/neo/groups/narcissisticabuse/conversations/messages/5458

Support groups for victims of narcissists and psychopaths (and one or two groups for narcissists)

http://dmoz.org/Health/Mental_Health/Disorders/Personality/Narcissistic/Support_Groups/

Return

After the Rain
How the West Lost the East

The Book

This is a series of articles written and published in 1996-2000 in Macedonia, in Russia, in Egypt and in the Czech Republic.

How the West lost the East. The economics, the politics, the geopolitics, the conspiracies, the corruption, the old and the new, the plough and the internet – it is all here, in colourful and provocative prose.

From "The Mind of Darkness":

"'The Balkans' – I say – 'is the unconscious of the world'. People stop to digest this metaphor and then they nod enthusiastically. It is here that the repressed memories of history, its traumas and fears and images reside. It is here that the psychodynamics of humanity – the tectonic clash between Rome and Byzantium, West and East, Judeo-Christianity and Islam – is still easily discernible. We are seated at a New Year's dining table, loaded with a roasted pig and exotic salads. I, the Jew, only half foreign to this cradle of Slavonics. Four Serbs, five Macedonians. It is in the Balkans that all ethnic distinctions fail and it is here that they prevail anachronistically and atavistically. Contradiction and change the only two fixtures of this tormented region. The women of the Balkan - buried under provocative mask-like make up, retro hairstyles and too narrow dresses. The men, clad in sepia colours, old fashioned suits and turn of the century moustaches. In the background there is the crying game that is Balkanian music: liturgy and folk and elegy combined. The smells are heavy with muskular perfumes. It is like time travel. It is like revisiting one's childhood."

The Author

Sam Vaknin is the author of Malignant Self Love - Narcissism Revisited and After the Rain - How the West Lost the East. He served as a columnist for Central Europe Review, PopMatters, Bellaonline, and eBookWeb, a United Press International (UPI) Senior Business Correspondent, and the editor of mental health and Central East Europe categories in The Open Directory and Suite101.

Until recently, he served as the Economic Advisor to the Government of Macedonia.

Visit Sam's Web site at http://samvak.tripod.com